I0479653

How to Build a Brand With Authenticity for Success

Volume 3
PR and Social Media, Costing and Production

Written by
Lisa Elliot-Rosas

Edited by
Eveline Morel
Bryce Brecheisen

ISBN: 9781675926482

DEDICATION

To all the brands out there that are open to growth.

CONTENTS

ACKNOWLEDGMENTS

The many brands I have partnered with over the years to bring growth and success.

A few to mention that have been true partners with team participation, empowerment and kindness are:

Mara Hoffman
Laura Odell from The Odell's
Emilee Dziuk at Gara Skincare
Corinne Grassini at Society for Rational Dress
Grey Ant

www.furoclothing.com

1 PR STRATEGIES AND SOCIAL MEDIA

1.1   Brand Communication Basics

The purpose of brand communication is to inform consumers about the brand and its activities as well as convince them that the brand's products are superior and more desirable than those of the competition.

Information happens at a rational level while reminding and convincing happens at both rational and emotional levels to create feelings and emotional associations.

Brands use communication to achieve its intentions through visuals such as images, photos, graphics, video, written communication like copy text and written words, and verbal communication such as radio, verbal endorsements, and video content.

1.2 Visual & Image Content - Photos, Graphic Elements & Video

The strongest and most effective means of communication to inform, remind, or convince consumers and wholesale buyers about a brand, is visual communication. A picture is worth a thousand words. Photos provide information about product details and its functionality. They also create brand identity or the 'feel' of the product.

Effective photos and videos can create an emotional reaction in the viewer and render a more powerful connection. Logos, colors, and brand symbols also reinforce the brand's image and help communicate its values.

At the consumer level, product images that evoke feelings and emotions are more effective. With wholesale buyers at the retailer level, product images that detail the product AND evoke a feeling are most effective.

The most important tools for communicating visual content for wholesale sales and retail buyers are the look books and line-sheets. Lookbook and line-sheets are the key to reinforcing brand identity and create a positive image of the brand in the wholesale buyers' minds. Keep in mind, however, that the image they develop of the brand is also often colored by their own preconceptions, priorities, values, and judgments. Lookbook and line sheets will be covered in more detail in a separate section.

1.3 Written Communication

A picture created through the words is just as important as a photo image. Words have connotations, cultural values, and certain associations. Words used as copy text can strengthen an image by highlighting the product's benefits and features that create value.

Written communication for wholesale sales is crucial. It creates value for buyers through listing a product's inspiration, blurbs, details, uniqueness, features, options, benefits, product and brand story. Written communication also helps to convince buyers of the brand's delivery promise to consumers.

It is also important to have unique and sought-after words and phrases in the subject matter of emails going out (whether a blast or individual emails). Sales is more than just selling; it is also how we market and communicate information about the brand.

In emails it is important to be short, factual and interesting to the customer you are communicating with. Give facts such as other strong stores, associated brand, and other key products the store carries. This will demonstrate your familiarity with their business and what is unique about your brand.

Written communication is often mixed with visual communication, in the form of fashion editorials, social media content, photographs, product marketing, sales materials, movies and video.

Don't Underestimate the Value of Typography and Fonts

How you say something is just as important as what you say.

If you produce quality content that gets traffic but can't seem to get readers to stay on your website, you may want to look at your text graphics and typography such font type and size. A text block that is not typographically structured will not sit well with many readers. Just like a spoon is a tool for getting food from your plate to your mouth, type is a tool for moving information off a page or website to a consumer's memory. When type design is good, the flow of information is smooth and satisfying.

Furthermore, typography can add emotion, drama and personality to the text and make it more visually appealing. It can subconsciously embed the message in the mind of the reader, and make it easier for them to understand, grasp and comprehend the presented information.

Emojis in emails can be effective showing a personal approach.

1.4   Verbal and Audio Communication

Verbal communication is also very useful for communicating about a brand. Verbal communication happens during product presentations, prospecting calls, telephone conversations. Verbal communication is often combined with visual communication, like movies, online videos, and slideshows with background music.

Sometimes playing a sequence of photos and a movie while associating it with a song is an effective way to communicate brand image. Verbal communication can inform and create emotional connections.

Don't Underestimate the Value of Sound

In a TED conference speech entitled "The 4 Ways Sound Affects Us" sound expert Julian Treasure outlines how sound affects people physiologically, psychologically, cognitively, and behaviorally. The same is true for visuals and performance. Communication elements can combine with sound to create the language of brand presentation.

Julian Treasure asserts in his talk that, "inappropriate retail soundscapes can reduce sales by 28%". If it's true in-store, it's also true on the web. Inappropriate dialogue, visuals and performance techniques can create a marketing and sales disaster.

Sound is more effective than images alone in reaching the nervous system to create an emotion and there are several studies to support the assertion. For example, the shower scene of Alfred Hitchcock's "Psycho" originally had no music until he asked his composer to write a score for that scene to increase the fear factor.

Music affects emotions more than images. Tempo and rhythm have physical effects on listeners. They can affect the heartbeat and cause other physiological reaction. Visuals alone cannot affect a person emotionally as much as sound. Even though light and sound both have wave properties, you cannot feel light in the same way that you can feel music in your body. Furthermore, music is more powerful than language at arousing emotions and crossing language and cultural borders. More than any other stimulus, music can conjure up images and feelings that need not necessarily be directly reflected in memory.

Though music appears to have similar features of language it is more rooted in the primitive brain structures that are involved in motivation, reward and emotion. The brain imposes structure and order on a sequence of sounds to create an entirely new system of meaning. The appreciation of music is tied to the ability to process its underlying structure and the ability to predict what will occur next in the song.

Music involves subtle violations of timing and because we know through experience that music is not threatening, these violations are ultimately identified by the frontal lobes as a source of pleasure. The expectation builds anticipation which, when met, results in a reward reaction.

Consider adding background music to your images or slideshows to add another dimension to your visuals and make your image (and brand) more memorable. You can also associate certain types of music and sounds with your brand on a permanent basis to cause brand association and differentiation. A great example is Verizon's 'pin drop animation accompanied by sound.

1.5   The Brand Elements that All Communications Must Reflect

Brand elements are tangible representations of the brand.

Logo & Other Design and Graphic Elements

Logos and other design and graphic elements are useful for creating a visual shortcut and a visual anchor for the brand. The logo must be representative and memorable. The rule less is more is always applicable.

Photos & Video Content

Product photos, alone and worn by a model or consumer, are very important. Depending on the type of product, photo content is equally important, in the creation of a stronger 'vibe' that will make your product come to life. A picture is worth a thousand words but only if it's the right picture. All details and consistency matter to the brand of a line in for styling, make-up, hair, accessories, background, product shots.

Descriptive Words and Marketing Arguments Used by a Brand to Describe Itself

The words and adjectives used to describe the brand are important. The choice of words is important. Words paint pictures and have different connotations and value associations. A story to associate with the brand may be more memorable and stick to the consumers' minds. It's important to use emotional marketing words to create communication that touches consumers and stays in their memory. Creating positive emotions that are associated with positive images and emotions is key.

Consistency of Photos, Wording, and Product for Strong Brand Definition

Photos must work together with your brand's written message. Your photos must create a perception that will take advantage of your brand's competitive strengths. Your logo, photos, and brand message should all work together to provide a strong message. Again, less is more and quality is more important than quantity.

Figure out the message and objectives and then refine each branding element to combine or re-combine for the strongest message. Test the elements on your target consumer and see what reaction you get and then refine and modify.

1.6   PR Basics

Public relations are defined as the external communication of a brand's message through editorial and non-advertising content that's non-paid to create more brand awareness and spread a brand's message.

1.7   Difference between PR and Advertising

There's an old saying, "Advertising is what you pay for, PR is what you pray for." Whereas Advertising is paid, PR is traditionally non-paid although that line is blurring more and more. Advertising is paid media and public relations is earned media. An example would be convincing reporters or editors to write a positive story about your brand to appear in the editorial section of the magazine, newspaper, TV station, or website, rather than pay for an ad in the advertising section where advertising. A story has more credibility when it is independently verified by a trusted third party rather than purchased.

1.8   PR is more Credible

PR has more credibility and influence because it's written by an expert or trusted third party. Consumers tend to trust someone that is giving their own opinion rather than an advertisement. However, they both have a place: ads can reinforce a brand image and keep the brand in the consumers' mind,

1.9   Advertising and PR both Cost Designer Money

In the end, brands need to pay for both advertising and PR. For advertising, you pay a media buying company or the media directly for running the ad and the marketing department of the brand or designer controls the message and appearance of the advertisement. For PR, the designer pays a publicist who contacts media and influencers for editorial placement. There is very little control of what the media chooses to say about the brand or how they say it when the story or editorial content appears.

1.10   Quick Cost Comparison - Advertising vs. PR

A good PR showroom will charge about $2,000 - $5,000 per month for editorial and celebrity placement. Annually the cost is $24,000 - $60,000 and averages about 10 to 15 media and celebrity hits, depending on the line.

An advertisement in a print fashion magazine with national circulation that appears for 1 month, costs anywhere from $10,000 – to $20,000. Online and Facebook advertisement may cost less but can still add up.

PR is more credible but often takes more work. It's important for a brand to understand their objectives and to choose the right PR activities that will bring the brand exposure and a good return on investment.

A recent study from 2014 by Nielsen commissioned by inPowered on the role of content in the consumer decision-making process concluded that PR is almost 90% more effective than advertising. "On average, expert content lifted familiarity 88 percent more than branded content..."

1.11   PR Activities - Overview

There are various PR activities that are generally used to attract media attention. It's important to remember that the target audience for PR activities is the media who in turn talk about the brands. It's important to remember the objectives of the media and what they want in order to get what you want, media coverage.

1.12   Fashion Shows and Fashion Presentations

Fashion shows, with their elaborate sound and light display, are more fashion theater where people go to see and be seen. They have traditionally been the way that brands show new collections. If there is an association with a show from the brand using accessories, then these brands should be credited in invites and pamphlets.

The fashion shows are geared towards the press, even if the photos from the shows are released online to consumers within hours of the show being finished.

The purpose of the fashion show is to communicate the brand's image and products in a vivid manner and provide more than just the visuals to create the emotion that the line is trying to convey. Fashion shows are then reviewed by the media in their publications.

Fashion shows are very much about who's attending the show. The more celebrity attendees the brands have in the front rows, the more the media will come to the show. The media attends for the celebrities as much as the designers. Some buyers also attend fashion shows but are generally less interested in the theater aspects than in touching and seeing the garments up close.

Having celebrity attendees adds additional brand association and strengthens the brand's image as a brand that is in demand.

Pros and Cons of Fashion Shows

Very few lines are sold at fashion shows, so fashion shows are not about sales. Buyers generally don't order off the runway, they must see garments up close to discover the color choices and other details.

Benefit of Media Coverage

The major benefit of having a fashion show is the potential media coverage. It's important that the venue organizing the fashion shows can garner media and press coverage for the designers. If the designer is organizing the show themselves, they should hire a PR company who can ensure that press, bloggers, and celebrities will be attending.

Disadvantage of Fashion Show is Expense

The major disadvantage of having a fashion show is the expense involved. Fashion shows cost between $5,000 to $80,000 for the location, production, models, and associated expenses. Depending on the timing and location, the press attending the show may not be the top press so your line may still get limited visibility and coverage. Overall, fashion shows for new brands have a very limited return on investment considering the cost.

Fashion Presentations - A Cost Effect Alternative to Fashion Shows

It's important to show garments on models as models bring clothing to life. Having a fashion presentation instead of a runway show is more cost-effective. Presentations are less expensive because they use less models and have no need for a runway and extensive lighting. They also allow more time for the models to show the outfits and for photos. Fashion presentations can also be more artistic in nature and can be part of larger installations.

A clever creative fashion presentation will provide the media more to talk about than a runway show that is not much different from other runway shows.

Should a Designer have a Fashion Show?

Fashion shows should be part of the marketing and communication budget. Depending on the sales revenue and how established the brand is, a fashion show might be expected. If you're a larger label and sell for hundreds of millions each year a fashion show is expected. For a relatively new brand whose sales revenue is less than $100,000, spending 1/5 of that ($20,000) on a fashion show may not be advisable. If you must show the collection to the media, organize a fashion presentation or private viewing as it will be more effective and less costly.

1.13   Editorial and Red-Carpet Placement

Another important PR activity consists in generating placement of items from the designer's brand in fashion editorial shoots published in print, online, and on red-carpet celebrity appearances that are photographed by the media. Again, the purpose of editorial and red-carpet placements is editorial coverage.

Fashion editorials can be very effective in inspiring the viewer by creating an emotional response and communicating a feeling. They help reinforce a brand by communicating an emotion to the viewer more than a runway fashion show review.

Fashion editorials are a form of media communication that target consumers. Like fashion shows, red-carpet placements are a great way for brands to get media coverage through association with celebrities wearing the brand.

The Intended Message of a Fashion Editorial may be Distinct from a Brand's Image.

In fashion editorials the way a brand is styled and worn by the model might not be consistent with the brand's overall image. The fashion editorial message may be different than the brand's message. It's important for designers and their agents to allow only editorial projects that are consistent with the brand's image or at least not hurt the brand image. For example, if your brand is about sustainability and non-violence having it photographed in an editorial with machine guns may not be a good association.

Red Carpet Placement Brand Visibility Depends on the Event and Celebrity

Red-carpet placement can be very effective in reinforcing brand image and creating brand awareness. The more well-known the celebrity/model, the more media exposure a brand **receives** when worn by that celebrity.

It's important that the association of the designer's brand with the celebrity's own personal brand be beneficial and useful. It's also important that the celebrity be sufficiently well-known to have enough media clout. If there is little media coverage the brand should consider the costs associated with placement to determine if it's worth the time and money invested.

Editorial and Celebrity Placement must have Accessible Samples

For editorial and celebrity placement, the designer's samples must be available for pulling or borrowing by stylists and costume designers. Most stylists like to group their pulling to a few trips and like having one-stop-shop locations where they can pull what they need.

PR showrooms, style houses, and even retail boutiques play a useful part in the process as they regularly communicate to the stylists and publicists to generate pulls, track samples pulled, and follow-up with stylists to get photos and media coverage which can be days to months after the pull. This takes a significant amount of coordination and organization to ensure photos and media coverage and samples are not damaged or lost.

1.14   TV Shows

Being featured on a TV show whose target audience is a match for the target audience of the product can be good brand exposure

Television is still important even if it watched less or in different ways than in the past.

Featuring products on TV shows or other videos has limited benefits. Most of the time a brand's logo and credits are not presented unless the show segment is covering the designer and the exposure of the brand to the public is extensive.

TV Series Can Be Used by Designers for More Media Exposure.

Having the brand featured in a TV series is great exposure for the brand, especially if the series is very successful. The brand may get credits at the end, though most people don't watch the credits. The designer can use exposure from TV shows as a 'news' item that can be provided to the media to get additional media exposure. TV series exposure can bring additional media coverage.

1.15   Press Releases & Direct Media Pitching

Another PR activity that can bring great media coverage in articles and news features is direct pitches to media fashion editors, writers, and news desks. This involves direct contact with the writers and editors to understand their editorial calendar, what they're writing about, and a highlighted angle that would fit their story. For example, in a 'green issue' focused on sustainability the writer could focus on the designer's use of sustainable fabrics and production methods.

Newsworthy Information that Media may find Interesting

Press releases are a good way to keep the press informed of newsworthy activities that the brand may be doing. Fashion events, features on TV shows, new collection releases, and other actions, could be considered as news bits that are worth talking about in the media.

Press Releases Increase Press Visibility

Press releases are picked up by many news feeds and are good ways to get additional SEO visibility for online Google searches. Having SEO visibility is useful for brands that are looking to sell online through their online store and demonstrates that a brand is relevant to the public and being talked about which can help establish selling confidence with retailers. Certain retailers such as Zappos, Amazon and others, buy once a store has strong search and analytics.

Press Releases are Relatively Inexpensive

Press releases are a relatively cheap way for a designer to get media coverage even if they don't have a publicist representing their line. There are free press release distribution sites that have various distribution at different price levels. It's important to have a well-written and well-structured press release that is in the required format. Overall, this is a good way for designers to get media exposure.

1.16   Social Media & Bloggers

The rise of online blogs and social media have created new opportunities for brands to get exposure to the public through individuals that have a large public following with many people that view their feed on a regular basis.

1.17   Blogs are the New Fashion Magazines

Social media and blogging have, to a certain extent, replaced some of the fashion media and magazines. Many blogs feature beautiful editorial photography of outfits or other fashion content. Fashion blogs are an influential source of information to consumers. The public, especially Gen X and Gen Z demographic groups, relate to the bloggers' interests and lifestyle.

1.18   User Generated Content is Important to Millennials

Whereas Generation X and Baby Boomers still tend to get their news more from traditional print media, Millennials tend to trust bloggers and user generated content on social media more, for their fashion inspiration. Millennials trust user-generated content for suggestions on which product to buy rather than traditional media.

1.19   Influencer Mentions Create Additional Brand Visibility

Fashion influencers are either bloggers or individuals with high followings on social media. Social media followings are people who like the content enough to subscribe to it. It's more advantageous to be featured on a fashion influencer or blog for the visibility to the public and direct endorsement of the brand by the influencer.

Traditional media channels have also become active in social media. This is another useful way for brands to connect to traditional media especially fashion editors and writers.

1.20   Gifting Bloggers

In order to get blogger coverage and mentions, it may be necessary for brands to gift bloggers the product or make it easy for them to borrow it. Many PR showrooms also work with bloggers who borrow items for their own fashion editorial shoots.

A blogger with hundreds of thousands of followers on Instagram and Facebook may charge for featuring brands and may require them to own that item. Bloggers and social media influencers may also require payment of an endorsement fee to cover a brand in their content.

1.21   Social Media and Instant Press Coverage

Given the instant ability to post high-visibility, bloggers and social media influencers have become the guests of honor at fashion shows and other fashion events. They can provide instant coverage and buzz through their posts that are followed by hundreds of thousands of consumers.

1.22   Social Media and Online Press as More Cost-Effective PR

If funds are limited, it may be more cost-effective for designers to target their PR spending on social media influencers and bloggers with audiences that match their target consumer instead of paying expensive monthly PR retainer fees. There is also more certainty that a piece will be published than with traditional media where you don't know if you'll get coverage until the news item is published. Social media also gives you a greater ability to quantify and track the number of people viewing the website or news.

The designer should weigh the costs for social media posts and gifting by influencers versus the costs of other PR activities and know the effectiveness of each activity in providing coverage.

1.23   Designers Building Create Their Own Social Media Influencer for Direct Public Access

Another benefit of social media is the ability for designers to become influencers themselves by building their own social media following. This takes some focus and a constant and consistent effort.

In order to gain a following of people interested in your content you must have compelling content. The photos must be beautiful, well shot, and aspirational. Viewers must be inspired when seeing the photos.

Content must be posted on a regular basis (at least a few times per week), and should reflect the brand's beliefs, lifestyle, and values. Content must add value to consumers for them to follow it.

1.24   Social Media Overview

Include an overview of social media channels, and main information to know about each channel.

1.25   Factors for Social media Success

- Have Clear Objectives
- Drive Action and Engagement
- Email Stimulates Action
- ID & Manage Active Users and Communities
- Go Where the Market It
- Be Relevant

- Listen to What is Being Said and Where
- Engage and Add Value to Existing Conversations
- Combine Offline & Online. Act Offline and Share Online

1.26 When and How Much to Pay for PR

The questions of how much to pay for PR and what type of PR activities are most useful is often raised with new and emerging brands. Many designers spend more money on PR than on sales and product sampling activities and have little results and sales growth. Ultimately, the effectiveness of PR activities must translate into the bottom line which is more sales.

If the designer has their own online store PR spending can help drive online sales and its effectiveness can be more easily measured. Driving traffic to an online store is easier than driving traffic into a brick-and-mortar location. Conversely, it may be easier for a brand to drive traffic to their own website and sell through that website than drive traffic to another retailer who may be selling the designer's goods along with other brands. PR is important for creating a brand image and is often seen as more credible as straight-out advertising or sales content. When it comes to PR versus advertising, PR is more cost-effective at building brand awareness. It is more advisable for designers building their brand to use PR rather than advertising.

However, advertising is still important for building and maintaining brand image for luxury brands. If a designer aims to be a luxury brand and their price-points are comparable to other designer and luxury brands, they will have to advertise and follow the same practices that other luxury brands do in order to be seen as competitive.

Depending on objectives, it's important for brands to determine what PR activity will bring the desired results in the most cost-effective and fastest manner.

PR should Provide Measurable Results to Justify the ROI

In order to justify the spending and to track the effectiveness of that investment, PR activities should have trackable and measurable results. It's important to measure what was achieved with each PR activity. Results can be tracked through social media likes and comments, followers gained, views (on YouTube), number of social media and blog posts, website traffic, press release views and click-throughs, and email click-throughs.

PR in Proportion to Brand Sales and Marketing Costs

PR costs should be in proportion to the brand's revenue and a portion of the brand's marketing costs. Based on industry statistics, marketing costs should not exceed about 30% of a brand's revenue.

It's important for designers to invest in marketing a brand but their investment in marketing and communication should be proportionate to their investment in sales and product development.

1.27   PR Crisis Management

Bad news is important to address as it travels fast. It's important for designers to pay attention to any negative posts about the brand. If it's a product issue tit must be addressed right away. Building a brand includes the actions that the company owning the brand takes. Do they stand behind the brand? Do they take care of the consumers? If the bad publicity has to do with associating the brand with other individuals or companies that are garnering bad press, brands should address the issue.

Bad news travels fast and sometimes faster than good news. It's important for brands to make sure that the bad news don't overshadow the brand. This is also relevant on comments on on-line stores from end consumers.

What is Negative PR?

Negative PR is most often associated with product quality, fit and actions that the brand is taking that are not popular with the public. Negative PR creates a negative brand image in the minds of consumers and associates negative elements to the brand that will likely hurt sales.

If the brand has its own brick-and-mortar stores and retail establishments, paying attention to Yelp and other ratings sites mentioning the brand is important to tracking any negative reviews. If the brand is sold on Amazon, paying attention to user reviews is important.

How to Deal Effectively with Negative PR

If there is any negative PR connected to product it must be addressed with the customer and the action must be publicly acknowledged. If it's related to another issue, in some situations, identifying a positive spin on the negative information or correcting the information through an official post or release is important.

Remember that the public has a short attention span and what may be big news one day will often be forgotten two days later. In this vein, a way to deal with negative PR is to add positive news items or actions that will ultimately shift the balance back to a positive image of the brand.

In some situations, it may be useful to consult a reputation repair company or other companies specifically focused in dealing with negative PR.

1.28   Case Studies

I have worked with the following clients that are succeeding with PR, Marketing, and Sales and creating brand names within the industry.

- Ace & Jig
- Mara Hoffman
- Iro
- Zadig & Voltaire

On-line presence: showing point of view specific to the brand/lifestyle

Social ads

Strong social following and engagement

Stories on behind the scenes and the designer, philosophy, values and processes to create the line.

Product shot on strategic celebrities and influencers and digital platforms and magazines

Newsletters weekly with catchy subject lines and interesting new news, expansion into new categories, opening of own stores

Own on-line e commerce with strong following and sales

End consumer following which creates demand for customers to ask for line at different retail stores

Excellent photos and product that are unique, cohesive and consistent for Press and Sales

Credit key stores in press received

Digital advertising with on-line retailers: ex: Shopbop and Revolve plus others

Garmentory or Farfetch featured on

Key bloggers known to promote the brand

Collaborations with larger brands

Events at retailers, on-line and other avenues to build the name and excitement

Using known actress/models in campaign and exhibiting this in marketing materials and blown up images at tradeshows

Community events and engaging with real customers

Sustainability, plus size and other news that is on trend, important and relevant

Videos and shows

Extra budget for marketing for on-line retailers and catalogs with majors.

1.29   PR Do's and Don'ts

Here are some common mistakes, and suggestions, when it comes to PR.

Do's

- Create specific objectives and media action plans to reach these objectives.
- The brand should have its own social media channels and post regularly. If the designer doesn't have the time to do this, use a social media maintenance company and/or individual to do this.
- Create budgets for PR activities and events and don't exceed these budgets.
- Review your PR activity and results quarterly and after each major activity.
- Follow up from PR events.

- Build a PR contacts list. This takes time but is a good investment. Even if a designer ends up having a publicist or PR showroom for PR management, brands should also build their own internal contacts.

- Be mindful of the brand image created through the PR communication. Stay consistent to maintain the same brand image and communicate the same values.

- Create compelling content and invest in creating content on a regular basis.

- Communicate not just about the product, but the 'why' and beliefs of the product to create trust.

- Explore sponsorships, co-branding, and other opportunities that allow the brand visibility at minimal costs.

- Compare costs and effectiveness of various activities and choose the most cost-effective one.

- Make sure that your fashion show is not at the same time as the fashion show of another major brand that has a lot of media coverage.

- Make sure your social media feeds presents a consistent brand image. Vary your social media posts depending on the media. Have a schedule before the week for all posts to create a continuous story.

- Tag stores, press, and bloggers in posts and have them retag you for a larger following.

Don'ts and Common Mistakes

- Don't spend money on a fashion show if the media coverage of past events organized by the same group is not enough. Check media coverage for previous events hosted by the same group before you sign the agreement. Request to see media coverage and press as they should be able to provide it.

- Don't spend on advertising at the expense of PR. PR is more measurable than advertising.

- May designers spend on photo and video packages for fashion shows, you may spend less and get more from having your own staff photographer cover the event.

- Don't spend any money on PR services without a written agreement of what exactly is being provided, by when, and how the results can be seen and measured. You may want to withhold the last portion of the payment until the final results are delivered.

- Don't gift to celebrities if you don't have a way to get a photo or post from them. This should be much easier with social media now.

- Don't spend money on celebrity gifting events unless you have good product signage for photos, a way to get photos with each celebrity getting your product, and the celebrity event attendees that are confirmed are A-or B-list celebrities with significant followings and media exposure.

- Don't post randomly to social media. Make sure that all your posts and photos create a cohesive, beautiful feed and vary your posts depending on social media.

2. COST MANAGEMENT FOR HIGHER PROFITS

2.1   Product Costing Basics: Materials, Labor, and Other Costs

To create a fashion line, it's important for designers to maintain strict controls of material and labor costs as they can affect the profit margin.

2.2   Costing Formula

Costing a Garment is a Mathematical Formula:

Costs of Fabric + Trims + Labor + Business Overhead + Profit = Garment Cost (COGS)

COGS

Costs of goods sold (COGs) includes all the materials and labor specifically required to produce the actual items ordered by the stores. This covers the obvious expenses tracked throughout production such as fabric, buttons, zippers, handles, fittings, lining, fusing, thread, labels, and hangtags. It also includes the labor costs for production patterns, marking, grading, cutting, sewing, packing, and shipping. Remember the costs of the specific hangers, ticketing, and shipping containers required by the retailers.

Indirect Costs

There are also indirect costs. These include design and development costs and general administrative costs.

Design and development costs include all the expenses of the sample collection like fabrics and first patterns. It also includes research and development expenses such as costs incurred on trips to fabric shows. Remember to account for your own labor if you make the patterns or samples or the pricing doesn't cover your costs when you start to outsource the work.

Obviously, the simplest garments cost less to make. As styling details like pockets, fancy seaming, linings and trims are added, the cost of the finished garment will also increase labor cost in production. If you have chosen an expensive fabric for one of your designs, it would be wise to keep the details to a minimum. Using expensive fabric and many styling details often makes the finished cost of the garment too high for the market for which it is targeted.

Overhead costs are affected by such factors as design research, markdown sales losses, brand advertising, promotions, rent, and everything else that goes along with owning and running a business. This all should be calculated into the costing of a garment.

General administrative costs include the costs of running the business, selling, and promoting the line. These include overhead for items like rent, bookkeeping, salaries, and telephone bills.

Sales expenses include items such as lookbooks and trade shows, advertising, and public relations. Markdown allowances, discounts, returns, and canceled orders are also sales expenses and, if they apply to you, must be included in your pricing.

Cost Allocation:

Cost of goods sold is attributed to each specific item. Design and development costs for sales and administrative costs need to be divided up and allocated across the entire collection. The process takes time, and designers become Excel wizards as they work to allocate costs correctly.

One of the biggest mistakes new designers make is not charging enough to cover their costs or provide for a profit. The price of a garment must cover the cost of goods sold, as well as all other indirect expenses.

If COGS are too High, Alter Garment Price Level

If the actual costs of the fabrics, trims, and design details of each sample are too high to result in a realistic and profitable wholesale price, the design will need to be altered to bring costs down. A designer may need to do the following to achieve a lower cost:

- Switch to a less expensive fabric
- Reduce fittings and trim
- Simplify the design
- Combination of all three

2.3   COGS, Wholesale Cost and Retail Cost

The cost of piece goods (fabric) is generally about one-third the initial production cost of a garment. For a small company the markup will be higher than for bigger mass-producing companies. Larger companies generally have a lower mark-up percentage due to the higher volume they manufacture.

Ultimately the final figures may be a subjective call of what the market will bear. If you price your garments higher than comparable garments sold in the same stores as your product, you will find that your clothes left on the rack!

Designing, for the most part, is experimental, and there will be a number of first samples that won't make it into the line. Editing the line or weeding out, is a very important stage that requires someone with experience to pick potential good sellers. The approved sample for the line should have the right combination of fabric, styling, and trims that can realistically be sold at the right price with an appropriate profit margin. It only takes a few good styles for a company to have a successful season. It also only takes a few bad styles to have an unprofitable season or even end an entire company.

Calculating wholesale price is not an exact science and can be complex. If you work with a sales representative, ask the rep to help you. Several pricing methodologies exist and one of the best approaches is to apply the same markup margin the retailer uses to the cost of goods sold. The markup will cover all indirect costs and provide the profit margin.

Retail pricing strategies vary by store. Generally, retail markup is double the wholesale price plus an additional 20% to 80% percent. This formula is often referred to as 2.2 or 2.8.

 Apparel is at the low end of the scale. Jewelry and shoes are at the high end. Markup can be as high as 3.0 for a product made in Europe to account for the extra cost of duty and freight.

To price a product with the same markup margin as the retailer (or 2.2 in this example) the math works like this:

Cost x 2.2 = Wholesale

Wholesale x 2.3 average markup = Retail

Some lines do a 2.2 markup, and some go up to a 2.5-2.6 to stay competitive.

At this stage, return to your research and determine whether the resulting retail price makes sense in the marketplace. If it seems too high, the wholesale price and COGS are too high. To save your margin you must find a way to simplify the item design, use less expensive materials, or gain production efficiencies with larger runs to bring down the COGS.

When manufacturing in Italy became too expensive, shoe designer Kristen Lee moved her production to Brazil to keep her pricing in line with the contemporary shoe market. Examine the resulting margin to determine if it is enough to cover your rent, salaries, and other fixed costs. If not, you may need to alter the COGS.

Generally, the goal is for pricing to leave roughly 15 percent net profit margin after all direct and indirect costs. In the end, it's not about the volume of product you sell, it's always about the margin. The only way to increase your margin is to increase your price or lower your costs.

The margin will increase as the business grows. The longer you are in business the more you will build in efficiencies that will decrease costs. For example, you will accumulate patterns that can be used again or adjusted by switching out sleeves or collars or you will meet the minimums for cheaper production and discounts in fabric and materials.

2.4   What's a Good Profit Margin?

Many designers ask what a reasonable margin target should be. The answer varies depending on the size of your business and its overhead, development, and sampling costs. Most companies try to achieve 50% margins at wholesale and over 70% in retail. Again, there are no hard and fast rules as each circumstance requires a different treatment.

2.5   Managing the Cost of Materials

Cost of materials includes fabric, notions, and other related fabric-treatment services. Choosing the fabric, materials, and trim is an exciting and critical part of the design process. It's the combination of textures, fabrics, materials, and trim that can create aspirational pieces that are more than simply clothes.

There are many sources of fabric and materials. Researching and reviewing the options can be overwhelming and choosing the right fabric is a business decision as much as an aesthetic choice. It's important to narrow the options by price, minimums, and lead times.

First Learn about Your Materials

Before you source the materials, learn about fibers, textiles, trims, and finishes. This will help you with the entire production process.

The content of the materials greatly affects the design results, and a designer should understand the behavior of different fibers like whether they stretch, whether the color or print is dyed or woven, and the attributes of natural versus synthetic fibers, and how the weave and weight affect the shape and durability of the product. Ideally, a designer should be able to feel a fabric and know if it is suitable for the design.

The best way to learn about fabric is through hands-on experience. Working at a fabric store such as Mood in New York is great training. It's well worth packing up a booth or working a few days in an office to acquire this knowledge

You can also learn by visiting a fabric show. Approach the fabric representatives in booths when they aren't busy and ask questions. People love to share their expertise if they have the time. A designer can also volunteer to help a fabric rep in exchange for fabric lessons.

Fabric Minimums

Most suppliers of fabric and trim have a minimum amount of yardage (or meters in Europe) that designers can order. The minimums exist because for the supplier, servicing, shipping, and selling small quantities is less profitable.

Each supplier has a different threshold of what quantities are worthwhile. Minimums can range from 15 to 5,000 yards but generally, for the designer fabric market, the average is around 300 yards. Certain fabrics from the same mill have different minimums depending on the content of the fabric, the finishes, or the print.

When you are new to the market and your orders are small, meeting minimums can be difficult. New designers do not need, nor can they afford, to buy excess quantities of fabric.

When approaching any source for fabric or trim, learn the minimums up front. Though this question will expose you as a little fish and possibly not worth the supplier's time. In my opinion, it's a waste of your time to discuss materials you cannot have. You do not want to fall in love with a sample fabric that you can't get to produce your orders.

What Happens if You Cannot Meet Fabric Requirements?

Sometimes new designers cannot meet the minimums required by fabric suppliers because they are not manufacturing big enough quantities with their initial orders. There are a number of ways to work with this.

Buy Sample Yardage

Generally, a supplier has two prices for fabric. One price is for sample yardage that is higher for a small amount of fabric that designers buy to create test samples. Another price is for production yardage, which is charged at a lower price charged for the larger quantities needed to produce store orders.

Sample yardage is 20% to 50% more expensive than production yardage because the quantities are small. However, if you cannot meet the required quantity for the production price, you can still purchase the entire amount you need at the sample price. The cost will be high and there is a risk as the mill won't work with you next season if you don't return for a larger production quantity.

Pay More Per Yard if Possible.

Sometimes a source will make a minimum exception if you pay more per yard or pay a fee. This is generally a much better deal than paying the full sample yardage price.

Many European mills have expensive, couture lines of fabric and because the fabric is expensive, the profit margin is higher for the mill and they will sell that fabric in smaller quantities.

You can also negotiate with the supplier to find other ways to get past minimums or keep your price down. Ask them if a major manufacturer is buying the fabric and can track your order on to the end of the larger order.

Buy Stock Fabric

Ask the mill or supplier what fabric it has in stock. Most places house a selection of fabrics that require smaller minimums. If they don't stock exactly what you want, like black lace for example, they may have white lace that you can dye.

They also may stock greige goods which are unfinished goods that can be quickly dyed or treated. Ask whether they sell off leftover fabric at the end of the season. If you do buy stocked fabric, find out how much they have in total because if they run out you may be back to facing a 300-yard minimum to fill orders.

Use Fabric that is Ready for Dying Use

Designers find other clever ways to deal with minimums. For example, if you offer a shirt in four colorways and the orders don't meet the minimums to buy the fabric in each color, you can buy the fabric for all of the shirts in white and dye it yourself. Just make sure the fabric can be dyed and remember to factor the dyeing cost into your cogs.

Have Your Production Factory Source Fabric

If planning to use overseas manufacturing in China or elsewhere, check with your factory to see if they can source the fabric for you.

Manufacturing Lead Time can Limit Fabric Options

Another factor that can limit your fabric options is lead time. This is the time it takes to receive the materials once you place the order.

Lead times vary. Some fabrics arrive in four weeks, but eight weeks is standard with mills and converters if the materials aren't in stock. The same applies to trims. Basic items such as zippers may be stocked but a special button or ribbon can take several weeks to arrive.

Large orders take precedence and your small order may be pushed to the end of the queue and cause unanticipated production delays and late store delivery.

Amanda Thomas, COO of Loeffler Randall said "the biggest challenge to delivering to the stores on time is the regular delays in receiving raw materials."

Large, established fashion brands have spent massive budgets on supply chain optimization technology and systems to save time and money on production. Plan carefully to know exactly how much lead time your production schedule affords and make sure that you always build in a cushion in case of problems.

Designer Gary Graham buys his fabric in Italy now but when starting out, he only bought domestic fabrics. He said, "Delivery is so important when you are new, you just can't be too much of a fabric snob."

Sit down with the sales agent and ask what you can receive in the least amount of time. Be sure to include shipping time in the schedule. It can take a week or more to get the fabric from the mill once it's ready.

Stick Within a Budget

Know your budget and stay within it! Fabric ranges widely in cost and expenses can escalate quickly if you let your creative side off the leash. Fabric can account for as much as 30% of each season's costs and the cost of each material also affects the final product price. Know in advance what you can spend while keeping your profit margin and creating items shoppers can afford to buy.

The fabric expense must make sense for the garment. Designer Nicole Miller explained the importance of fabric quality and price making sense to the end consumer, "It has to look like the money. You can buy a plain linen for $25 per yard or you can buy a beautiful evening fabric for $25 per yard. You can get the money for the evening dress, but you won't for the linen, because no one can tell a nice linen from an average linen."

If you use an expensive fabric on an intricate garment with complicated construction, tailoring, or pleating, the high fabric cost will add to the high production cost, potentially resulting in a market price too high to sell.

To keep the cost of the final garment reasonable, expensive fabric should be used for simple designs that cost less to cut and sew. Designer Gary Graham offers an option to buyers when using expensive materials. If he is using a $21-per-yard jersey for a dress, he will offer the dress in a $3.50-per-yard cotton ribbing as well.

The quality of material must also be consistent throughout the product. Don't make the mistake of the evening wear designer who lined a silk charmeuse gown with polyester.

Limit Yourself to Fewer Fabrics

For the first few seasons this will help you keep down expenses and meet minimums. A fabric can be used in multiple designs and still look fresh to the buyer and customer. For example, the same silk chiffon will look completely different in an evening dress versus a playful tank top. It can be lined or unlined, crinkled, pleated, flat, or bias cut and mixed with different trims.

Don't Order Excess Fabric

Over ordering wastes money and results in inventory that the designer needs to sell at a discount or throw away. Excess fabric eats up so much money and you are left with fabric you can't use. Even if a fabric is only $2.50 a yard and you buy 20 yards, you may only get enough orders to use 10 yards, which means your fabric really cost you $5 per yard because you must factor the cost of the excess into your overall expense. Unfortunately, when you do resell leftover fabric to a jobber, you often receive as little as 1/30th of the price you paid.

Of course, if you have a strong season and have to repeatedly reorder small quantities of fabric at the higher price to fill reorders from the stores, you will also be wasting time and money. With experience, you will learn to anticipate reorders for certain items and order the fabric in advance but when starting out with limited funds it's not worth the risk.

Don't Order Fabric Until You are Sure

Wenlan Chia, who designs Twinkle, makes her fabric decision early in the design process. She looks at swatches and doesn't sample fabric until she knows it will definitely be in the collection. Michelle Smith of Milly, designs her entire collection off the swatches and even finalizes her silhouettes before ordering fabric.

Always Confirm Price and Payment

When you are ready to order, clarify the price for sample fabric, a full roll (generally 60 to 80 yards), and production quantities. Make sure you get the best price available for the quantity you need and don't be afraid to negotiate. Read the fine print and work out delivery details and payment terms up front.

Most fabric suppliers require prepayment or cash before delivery (CBD), payment in full on a credit card, or at least a deposit with the balance due cash on delivery (COD). Once you establish credit or build a relationship with the vendor, you can ask for net 30 terms, which give you 30 days from when the fabric is shipped before you have to pay.

When buying imported fabrics, confirm the price currency. There is a big difference between US $8 per yard and €8 per yard. Fabric from Europe is sold by the meter, adding yet another variable. When the U.S. dollar declines in value, U.S. designers should keep an eye on the exchange rate. If the dollar falls by 5 percent, the fabric cost increases by the same percentage and it may be necessary to source your materials elsewhere.

Designing your own prints is very expensive. If you do create a custom print, understand that each color adds to the cost. To save expense, keep the number of colors per print down and then create the print again in different colors to get more use from it.

Check Fabric for Damages Prior to Cutting

Once the sales representative starts writing orders the manufacturer will begin to write cutting tickets. This will give a good idea of the items in the line will and will not be good sellers. An estimate of the yardage will then be made, and the fabric ordered. As soon as the fabric arrives for production it must be checked for flaws or shading. If this is done as soon as the fabric is received there may be enough time to return and replace any damaged fabric.

Don't Order Too Much Fabric

As soon as the line is completed, duplicates are made for the sales reps to show to buyers. An estimate of how much fabric will be needed to produce the line is usually done at this time. This step should be given close consideration. Ordering too much fabric will result in waste and will take away from the profit. Ordering too little fabric will result in losing orders and profit margin.

These days it is best to be conservative and to order on the safe side. If there are more orders and not enough fabric, you can explain the problem to the retailers, who may be willing to wait for a reorder of fabric to fill their orders.

Don't Forget to Factor in all other Fabrics

Facing and interfacing fabric, quilting fabric, lining, and other fabrics that may be included in the production of the garment should not be forgotten. Likewise, tear-away fabric that may be needed for sewing and embroidering delicate fabrics needs to be accounted for in the cost.

Notions & Accessories: Less is More

Decide how much trim is necessary and how it will affect the cost of your garment. In many situations, it's important to go back to the design and see what it is about. Is it about the styling lines, the detailing and stitching or the print? Is it about the trim?

Designers often pile on a multitude of elements, when they could do with much less. Prints, plus trim, plus stitching, plus a complex design, altogether make for a cacophony of elements that fight for attention and create an overloaded design that lacks strong focus.

It's time to prioritize on the design story and remove extraneous elements. Practice less is more. What would happen if you removed some elements? Consider minimums for notions and accessories and lead times.

Labels and Hang Tags

The company label, the size label, the fabric content and care labels required by Federal Trade Commission regulations must be sewn into the garments. Care labels must include complete instructions for regular care of the garment including information about bleaching, ironing, drying, and warnings if the garment cannot be cleaned without harm.

Labels must state the country where the garment was made if made outside of the United States. Complete information about labeling requirements can be found at www.ftc.gov in a document entitled "Threading Your Way through the Labeling Requirements under the Textile and Wool Acts."

If you sell to other countries be certain of their labeling requirements. For example, Canada requires bilingual content in both English and French.

Garment Add-Ons

Depending on the type of clothing and expected quality standards, it may be necessary to plan for hanger straps for strapless dresses and hanger appeal or extra button bags, etc.

Fabric Treatments: Dying & Digital Printing

Sometimes designers fail to include the fabric treatment in the cost of materials. Examples of fabric treatments are dying, washing, aging, stone-washing, and other processes it may have to go through before or after sewing.

Digital printing also adds cost to the fabric. It's important to get the production cost for digital printing and learn how it varies across different base fabrics and the quantity breakdowns.

2.6   Labor & Other Services

Labor and other services include the various inputs that go into producing the garments.

Patternmaking & Grading

For garments to sell, sizing must be correct and consistent from season to season. Unfortunately, there are no standard measurements for size. The basic guidelines are based on a 60-year-old study by the U.S. Department of

Commerce.

Not surprisingly, manufacturers have started using their own systems. In fact, sizing became marketing driven when manufacturers realized that a woman who is a size 10 is much happier if she fits into a garment with a size 8 label. Sizing, however, does need to relate to general consumer expectations, or it will be left in sales bins. The most important thing is to be consistent from season to season. Basic sizing guidelines can be found on websites such as www.fashiondex.com.

Grading is the process of adjusting the production pattern up and down to meet the sizes that were ordered. Grading is often offered by the factory or contractor and there are grading services that specialize in this work. Grading is charged per pattern piece and affected by the complexity of the pattern. Although it is usually too costly for new designers some recommend testing the grading and fit by making samples of a full-size range before continuing production in order to avoid delivery problems.

A Good Marker Will Save Time

Marking determines the best layout for cutting pattern pieces from the fabric.

A good marker will save time, eliminate fabric waste, and help you determine exactly how much fabric you need. Depending on the number of garments produced, a quarter inch of fabric saved by a good marker can eventually save yards of production fabric. The marker ensures that the pattern pieces are properly laid out with the grain of the fabric and can accommodate any patterns in the fabric. A new marker is created for each size in the range.

Production Patterns

Once you are ready for production, the factory will create the production pattern. This pattern is made from the sample but includes modifications made during sales to perfect the fit, design details, sewing guidelines, as well as, eliminate fabric and trim waste. A slight change in the seam allowance can save significant cost in production.

Once the line is edited and the sales representative has the line, then the first pattern is made into a production pattern. The production pattern is a perfected first pattern. This means that the first pattern is corrected for fitting and sewing details and the lay of the fabric is tested for an economical marker. The production pattern is then given to the Grader and

Marker Maker to be graded into sizes. These days the computer is mainly used to perform these two steps though there are still hand graders and marker makers who do an excellent job.

Grading is taking the first production pattern, which is normally a middle size, like a size 8, and grading it up and down into other sizes. Grading is an important part of production so the grader must be experienced.

Production Sample

If the factory didn't make a sample earlier in the process you will have it create one. Meet to inspect the production sample and discuss changes, quality concerns, scheduling, and specific costs. Factory managers are busy so you will want to utilize their time and expertise.

Ask them for their concerns about the samples and the overall job. The production samples that you agree on set the standard to monitor quality during production. Communicate that all units should be produced from the specifications and processes accepted on this sample and will be rejected otherwise.

Production samples of these graded sizes are sometimes made to test the fit and specifications are written for each garment and each size. This ensures that during production the garments are sewn exactly as the approved production samples.

Duplicate samples are usually made at this stage. Duplicates of the line, called sales samples, are sent to the various sales representatives to show to buyers all over the country. The larger the company, the more sales reps you have representing you, and the more sales samples that will be required.

The Grader usually makes the marker as part of their service. The marker is made for the complete pattern, using as little fabric as possible and interlocking the pattern pieces together to ensure there is no wasted fabric. It is printed onto paper that is the same width as the fabric. The marker is used by the cutter who will follow it while cutting out the pattern pieces. It is then laid over layers of fabric that have been rolled out onto large cutting tables. The fabric is sometimes rolled out and layered to thirty layers of fabric or more.

Cutting & Sewing

Having in house cutting demands higher sales volume to justify the cost of employing a full-time cutter. Therefore, start-up businesses usually give the fabric to a cutting service to cut the garments. Often, the cutter and the contractor are under one roof and will be responsible for both cutting and sewing the complete garment. The cutting is done on large, long, cutting tables that are the full width of the fabric rolled out onto them. The paper marker is placed on top of the fabric and the piece goods are then cut for production with band knives that vibrate up and down to cut through the numerous layers of fabric at one time.

Larger manufacturers use computers to grade, make the marker, and cut out the pattern from the fabric. The cut garments are then separated and bundled into lots to be sewn together by the sewers.

Usually the fabric is spread on tables and cut in large stacks. Make sure pieces from the same dye lots are cut together or the pieces within one garment may not match. Once cut, the pieces are bundled together with the thread, trims, and other items ready to be sewn.

Sewing and Production

Usually the contractor is responsible for taking the cut goods and sewing the garments for production. Larger companies sometimes have their own in-house sewing operators and yet will still contract out some of the work. Certain larger companies cut in the U.S. and then ship the cut garment to an offshore contractor to sew together. They may also have the total production produced abroad which enables the manufacturer to produce at a more competitive price point.

There are pros and cons for producing offshore. Some manufacturers would rather pay more and have their garments produced domestically to retain tighter control over the quality of goods, have a faster turnaround in production, and bypass customs and shipping costs. Contractors generally work in piece goods. This means the garment is sewn piece by piece. For example, one operator is responsible for sewing a collar while another is responsible for setting the sleeves and another completes the whole garment by sewing the finished pieces together. Each worker is paid depending on the number of pieces he or she has sewn.

Operators who show exceptional ability are frequently promoted to produce the first sample and responsible for the prototype samples. This Sample Hand position requires a person with many years of experience who can produce a good-looking garment. They are generally assured steady employment and a regular weekly salary.

A good sample maker is hard to find and well respected. Better wear companies have their garments sewn completely by one operator to assure a better-quality garment. These operators are paid by the hour and not by each piece produced. It is a common practice these days for a group of operators to be responsible for one garment and work as a team to sew the complete piece. This creates a sense of pride in the operators as their finished product is recognized as their own work. This is known as the modular method.

Other Outside Services: Pleating, Studding, Beading, Laser-Cutting and Garment Finishing

Sometimes it may be necessary to send out specific production processes to specialized contractors, especially if the production is done domestically. If using pleated fabric, this work is generally done by specialized contractors with specialized machinery. Same goes for embroidery, beading, laser-cutting and other garment finishing or embellishment. Overseas factories may be specialized in some of these processes or may have a lot of the machinery in-house.

2.7   Full-Package Production vs. Multiple Contractors

Production of garments can either be done in one place or between different places who each specialize in a particular task such as patternmakers, cutters, sewers, and finishers. The choice between a full-package production and using multiple-contractors depends on the number of garments being produced and the size of the factory.

Advantages and Disadvantages of Full-Package Production

Production can be simplified by choosing a vertical factory that offers multiple services such as fabric selection, patternmaking, production, and shipping, all at one place. Having fewer organizations involved means less opportunity for things to go wrong and processes to run late. The designer has more control, and because one factory handles many steps of the process, it is more likely to provide accurate cost and timing estimates up front.

Consolidation results in efficiencies and savings. Factories that order fabric and trim place orders for multiple brands, resulting in bulk discounts, particularly with standard fabrics, such as denim, and performance fabrics for swimwear or active wear. Designers don't have to run to the factory every time it is short a button because the factory sourced the button and can order more.

Many overseas factories offer packages that include the entire process from sourcing and sampling to producing, finishing, and shipping the goods. Increasingly in New York, if you ask for a full package, the factory will comply. However, while packages make the production management job easier, some designers feel that packages limit the choice of materials and process too much, leaving less room for maintaining quality standards and process control.

Advantages and Disadvantages of Small-Contractor Production

Every day, young designers in New York are seen schlepping from place to place just to complete one garment. They carry the fabric from the cutter, to another place for marking, to another for sewing, and then wait in line for an hour or more elsewhere to have the buttons put on. Transportation from one place to another can be tedious and expensive and the designer must manage the flow between vendors and contractors.

Consolidation is not always available and it doesn't always make sense. Many of the best factories only offer cut, make, and trim (CMT). They cut the fabric, sew each item, and trim by pressing, tagging, hanging, and packing for shipment. The other steps of the process, such as marking and grading, need to be outsourced. In some cases, the best sewers for the fabrication might be in a sewing room that doesn't offer other services, or the designs may require a cutter or sewer with special equipment. Sometimes it's simply less expensive to cut certain quantities in a cutting room or to hire an independent grading service.

Production Alternatives

Here are some production alternatives to consider.

In-House Production

Several emerging designers produce all, or at least part, of their line in-house with a small team that usually includes a patternmaker and a few sewers. Obviously, this method can be very expensive and requires a significant outlay of funds for cutting, sewing, and pressing equipment, as well as the permits, insurance, and licenses legally required to run a production facility.

A designer I know with a very small in-house sewing room spends $20,000 a month to keep it running. She says it's worth the extra expense because of the control it gives her. With in-house production, the designer can oversee the entire process every day and manage the timing and quality of each garment as it's produced. There is no competition from other designers and it's easy to react quickly for reorders and work around missing materials.

Designer Gustavo Cadile couldn't meet the minimums at the beading factories for his intricate evening wear gowns, so he manages an in-house team of extremely talented and experienced couture sewers who handle all his beading, sample production, and special orders.

Producing in-house results in a tight team of people who learn to work together efficiently. This gives the designer an opportunity to train and teach the team to become experts in signature fits and finishes. Some designers take sewers on field trips to high-end stores like Saks Fifth Avenue, to study the technique and finishing of different garments and set expectations.

An in-house sewing room can help protect proprietary information about design and fit. A designer told me she sends out her jackets, blouses, and dresses to a factory but will never contract out her pants. She has worked tirelessly to develop a signature fit, and with many other jobs moving through the factories, she doesn't want to risk someone stealing her pattern.

In recent years, many New York factories have shut their doors, leaving a number of highly skilled workers out of a job. These are ideal people to hire for in-house production. Keep in mind, however, that even with your own in-house team, you won't have all of the special skills required for each collection and will still have to contract out specialty work such as beading or knitwear.

In-house production requires you to be there every day with the sewers, directing them and reviewing their work. Some designers who have an intense focus on quality are happy to spend all day measuring seams and checking finishes to ensure that each item is consistent. But not every designer wants the time-consuming responsibility of managing manufacturing processes and people.

A full-time production staff brings additional pressure. The sewers are employees and bring a serious financial obligation in terms of their salaries and benefits. You need to have work to keep them busy and if the business fails, you won't be the only one left without a job.

Freelance Sewers

If your orders are small or require special skills, individual sewers (or craftspeople) can be hired on a freelance basis to handle the production. Freelance sewers are expensive and generally take longer to produce but they can be the best option when filling a one-time order for a store or creating specialty items that require detail or handwork. However, if you anticipate a large reorder or increased business with the store, you should get a factory involved to keep the production quality consistent on all runs and to provide quantity discounts and cost-effective measures.

Patch NYC started its business with a collection of crochet hats made completely by the mother of one of the designers and then embellished by designers John Ross and Don Carney. John said, "after one especially crazy crochet season, we realized Mom just couldn't keep up. We brought in two of Don's aunts and one of Mom's friends to help that season. Suddenly, there were all these variations in the hats since each person crochets slightly differently. We stopped wholesaling the crochet hats and only added knits back into our collection seasons later when we found a factory that would produce quality hats and scarves.

Nathalie Alabama Chanin, the designer of Project Alabama, returned to her hometown of Florence, Alabama, to find quilting circles that could supply the handwork needed to produce her T-shirts. She supports the hometown economy by subcontracting to more than 100 women to do the stitching.

2.8   International Offshore Production

International, offshore production is often seen as a cheaper alternative. Most of the clothing is made overseas due to labor costs.

Costs Associated with Offshore Production

When producing offshore, designers need to consider the following production factors that can add to production costs.

Shipping

Even with inexpensive labor, producing overseas can cost as much as producing domestically because of shipping. Sending materials to the factory and having it send product back to you is expensive. Designers also spend to send samples back and forth numerous times during the production cycle to monitor quality. For each shipment, duty and taxes must be paid.

Exchange Rates

Designers who produce overseas follow the exchange rates daily because of how greatly they affect their costs. Always confirm in which currency you are dealing. The recent high valuation of the euro versus the U.S. dollar has been challenging for many American designers who produce in Italy.

Shoe designer Kristen Lee stated that part of her reason for moving production out of Europe was because the exchange rate was pushing her wholesale pricing out of the contemporary market where her product is positioned.

Terms and Minimum Quantities

Minimums are generally high at overseas factories and many of them require you to have a line of credit. Most international factories expect a 50% down payment with the remaining 50% percent due at customs.

Offshore Production

Designers generally choose to produce overseas for either cost or quality reasons. Italian factories are credited with producing the highest quality of designer goods. They understand designer clothes and have highly trained craftspeople and artisans who have learned from generations of experts and take pride in their work. As a result, buyers are often more interested in items made in Italy.

Other countries have specialties too. Beading in India, knits in Peru, sweats in Canada, embroidery and other skills in Mexico, Turkey, Africa, and the Caribbean.

China has taken a great share of the market from these countries. Asia is credited with the cheapest production because of low labor costs. In the last few years, China and Hong Kong have responded remarkably well to small companies. The myths that the factories in Asia are not interested in small designers and that their quality isn't as good are no longer true.

There is a wide selection of factories in terms of size, quality, and expertise. There are factory owners who care about the quality and the vision for the product. Most emerging designers produce their knits in China because Chinese factories offer convenient packages and there are no longer as many knit producers in New York.

Recently, there has been some consumer backlash against goods produced in China, which affect sales to a select group of customers. Reports of high levels of toxins such as formaldehyde in clothing and fabric, have created apprehension about the Made in China label, especially in the children's wear market.

Communication Considerations when Producing Offshore

Although communication may not directly affect profit margin, it can indirectly have an effect: you may need to have a translator, r local-language speaker. Communication limitations could cause delays and production problems.

Language

Even if your contacts speak English, little misunderstandings from language differences can cause big production problems. If you don't know the language where you produce, communicate clearly and take extra care to ensure that you understand each other. You may need to hire a production manager who is fluent in the local language or at least find an intern with the necessary language skills.

Training

It's important to train the overseas factory to make sure it thoroughly understands how the product should look and fit. Don't take anything for granted. If the people who work in the factory wear saris most of the time, you can't expect them to immediately grasp the tailoring details in the patterns or the importance of grain lines.

Timing

Holiday schedules. Most countries have more national holidays than the United States. European factories are generally closed for the entire month of August when womenswear designers are finishing Fall production as well as Spring samples.

In fact, as New York Spring fashion week creeps closer to August, Italian factories are starting to feel the pressure to cut their traditional holidays or lose some of their larger customers to Asia. China and Hong Kong have several festivals throughout the year during which businesses close for at least one week. Designers should allow for this time in their production schedule.

Lead Times

Overseas production can take twice as much time as domestic production. Designers should pad their schedules to ship materials and patterns early and prevent late deliveries. Customs paperwork can cause delays and duties need to be paid.

Samples from Europe can arrive too late to make critical trade show dates. One menswear designer who was participating in his first New York runway show received only part of his collection when several boxes were delayed at customs. He was forced to send several models onto the runway wearing shirts and jackets with only underwear but fortunately pulled it off with good styling.

Culture

The working practices and customs in each country are different, and people in other countries don't work at the same fast pace as workers in the United States or Asia. Countless designers have told me about the frustration of getting work done in Italy where it always seems to be time to break for lunch. A designer needs to schedule extra time to avoid late deliveries.

Quality

It is more difficult to control the quality of production when you are thousands of miles away. Most large manufacturers have full-time employees who travel to or live in the production country to oversee the factory every day. New designers generally can't afford to do this and must work with an agent or have the factory send samples at several stages of the production process for approval. This takes time and if there are problems with the final product when it arrives, a local factory will need to fix it quickly.

Considerations for Choosing a Factory

Take the time to meet with several factories and choose one that gives you confidence. This should be done well in advance of your first sales season. This is a critical relationship. You will deal with these people often and need to trust them.

Some factory owners care about the quality of their work and the success of the line while others only care about completing the job and getting paid. When meeting the owner or manager of each factory, try to get a sense of the person, his priorities, and whether he takes pride in his work. There are several types of questions to ask so don't be afraid to look around and ask as many questions as needed.

Expertise and Specialty

Each factory has areas of expertise with the corresponding equipment and knowledgeable workers. Factories that excel at knits might not be able to produce outerwear or leather goods. Factories used to working with cotton or wool may not be competent with delicate silks. If a collection includes leather jackets, knit dresses, and woven pants, the designer may need to work with three different contractors.

It is also important to know what type of garments each specializes in and their price levels. If they mostly produce low-cost, mass-merchandise garments and your garments are higher-cost, contemporary garments, they may have the machines but not the experience to work at that quality level.

Types of Machinery Available and Production Services

Find out which production services the factory provides and whether they subcontract work out to other companies or do it all in-house. Many factories offer multiple services to attract more business, but subcontracted work is difficult to oversee. If you don't think the subcontractors can handle a process effectively don't give them the job. Do they have all the grading technology and machinery? Do they have various sewing machines with different needles for different fabrics?

Delivery

Ask if the factory regularly meets deadlines and establish the lead time for each job. Show your contact a sample or ask her to have one made to estimate timing as accurately as possible.

Inquire about the turnaround time for reorders. Reorders should be finished faster than the initial run.

Confirm what the factory means by delivery. To some it means the product left the plant or is on a boat, but you need to know when it will be in your possession.

What recourse will you have if the factory is late in delivering the goods?

Customer Service

- Find out whom you will deal with every day and how the factory ensure quality at each stage of production.

- See some of the factory's finished work to analyze its quality.

- Ask the factory owner how to lower your costs and improve the production process.

Credibility

- How long has the factory been in business?

- Who are some of its clients and how long have they been clients? Call these clients for a recommendation.

- Visit the factory and ask for a tour. Nancy Caton of Nancy Whiskey and the Sewing Factory advises, "Look for signs of good working conditions. Is the factory clean? Can you walk through it or is the fabric stacked up to the people's shoulders? Do the people look happy?"

- If you doubt that the factory is legal, ask to see its business license and watch for signs of labor abuse.

- How many employees are at the factory? Find out the factory's history of employee strikes and its policy if a strike causes production to stop.

- What happens if your goods are damaged at the factory or during transport? What kind of insurance does the factory have?

- Get a sense of how trustworthy the factory is regarding copyrights and private information. Probe the factory owner about other clients to see if the owner tells you things, he shouldn't. If proprietary details about another customer are shared, the owner will likely share the same information about you.

- Ask the factory to make a finished production sample after you receive the cost estimate but before you give that factory the job. This will help you judge the quality of the work and help the factory owner provide you with an accurate price. Making a sample helps the workers understand the piece and will give you a sense of what it is like to work with them. At this point, they want your business and will be as responsive as they can be. Some factories, mostly overseas, will create the sample for free to try and secure your business, but as explained earlier, others will charge you three times the production price out of fear that you are using them just to get a sample.

Price and Payment Terms

Unfortunately, the cost of production often ends up being the last concern for a young designer. In the panic of finding the right materials, contracting quality production, and trying to get product delivered on time, a designer will pay almost anything.

Before you contract with a factory, the factory should give you an initial cost estimate made from the sample or spec sheet. The greater the quantity of items produced, the less each item will cost. Everything is negotiable but if the price seems too good to be true, revisit any concerns about quality and delivery.

Generally, you will pay the factory COD with a deposit of at least one-third of the total price up front. Some factories require progress payments as the job passes through different stages of production. If a factory has had bad experiences with small designers, they may demand full payment in advance.

Pay fabric and production people on time and they will help you with discounts, better terms, flexibility on minimums, and other issues. The more work you give them, the happier and more supportive they will be in terms of price and service.

Pricing terms specify which party covers which parts of shipping. FOB includes the transportation to the shipping port but not the shipping, duty, or other costs from that point on. CIF includes shipping but not duty. When shipping fabric, ask for LDP in which the shipping and duty is included in the quoted price.

The Agreement

The written agreement should include pricing and the number and description of articles covered by the contract. Some of the contract items are:

- Delivery date
- Repercussions if delivery is late
- Detailed finishing
- Packing and labeling instructions according to the store requirements
- Shipping method (local messenger, trucking, sea, or air)
- Payment due date
- Method of payment

Before you begin, confirm the number of units to be produced, which stages of production will be handled by which contractors, and that all samples, materials, and patterns will be returned to you. Be very clear about the delivery date. Larger jobs take priority at factories and despite your contract it's smart to give them early deadlines to be safe.

Regardless of this contract advice not everything is written down. As one designer said, "Italian factories won't work with contracts unless your name is Prada, Gucci, or Ferragamo. You have to rely on the word of many people and be prepared for things to change without a moment's notice."

Advantages and Disadvantages of Offshore Production

It takes time and experience to learn how to manage production. Many factory owners and industry experts advise designers who want to have their own line to spend a few months in an internship or job at a factory. While students prefer to intern in the design room or even the production area of a big company, a few gritty months in a factory will provide a wealth of useful experience and knowledge. One factory owner said, "If you don't know anything, how can you tell anyone what to do? You need to know how to manage people, pinpoint problems, and identify mistakes."

Amanda Thomas of Loeffler Randall loves spending time in the factory. She says, "People in the factory love to teach and will take you around and show and explain processes to you. This is so helpful to production, and it is key in an organization to have someone who thinks like a manufacturer. A designer should learn this and be interested in this. If you want to make things you should learn how they are made."

It shows in the construction and quality of a garment when the designer has experience with the engineering and production process. Designer Bruno Grizzo noted that it was on his first job, working in the factory of made-to-order designer Frank Tignino, that he received an invaluable education on how to make clothes. He still works out of Tignino's spacious Garment District atelier, benefiting from a family-like relationship with his manufacturer.

When you work with a factory, be specific and communicate clearly and often. Don't be afraid to ask questions but don't be difficult or annoying. You need the factory's patience if materials are late or cutting tickets change during production because of new or revised orders. Know what you need before you call or show up and if there is a dispute, sit down and work it out calmly.

It may be necessary to train the sewers on each garment. In most factories each worker focuses on just one part of the garment, sewing just the side pant seam or sleeve inset before the garment is passed on to the next sewer. They don't always have a sense of the entire garment and final product. Even if you personally trained the team leader on your job, if a rush order comes in from a bigger brand, the lead sewer could get pulled off your job and leave less-trained workers to handle the remaining production.

Ana Beatriz produces her high-end womenswear line, Lerario Beatriz, in Brazil. She has a talented, full-time production manager located there but production is still constantly stressful. Each garment and process has to be carefully watched for quality and to avoid retail returns. She chooses to work with a small factory in Brazil where she specially trains a small group of five to seven workers specifically on her fabrics and techniques. She also has all her intricate embroidery handled through a non-profit organization that helps abused women make a living in embroidery.

Relationships are everything and designers such as Duckie Brown work with factory owners who have become important mentors. Some designers have received financial support from their factory and, in some rare cases, even produced the designer's sample collection for the runway at cost.

Increasingly, factories are looking to partner with smaller labels and even invest in their businesses. Many Chinese companies are seeking opportunities to continue their growth and increase their market shares. They seek to partner, produce, and help fund new labels. As larger manufacturers move production to Asia, Italian and other European factories are becoming more flexible. Rather than simply working with small labels they also offer to invest in them for increased efficiency, profit, and future loyalty. Manufacturers in places such as India often seek designers to create their own lower-priced lines and will partner to do your production in exchange for your design skills.

Thought you might feel desperate to find a factory to do your work, finding the right one is essential. If you don't like its work or you aren't comfortable with the operation, find another factory.

A designer should catch mistakes as they are happening and before the product is complete. Workers are paid by the piece. Their incentive is not to be careful but to be fast. As they speed up, they may take shortcuts that impact quality. If you show up regularly at the factory, they will take more care with your garments and work more slowly. At a minimum, check on the work during the beginning, middle, and end of the production run.

Return phone calls immediately. The factory should call you when things go wrong or if something doesn't look right. If your factory calls you for every concern, consider yourself lucky because others will only call once for every ten mistakes. Call back immediately. If the factory needs you, get there as soon as possible. Sometimes designers must go to the factory four times a day to deal with problems. Factory owners report that 95% of small designers don't call back right away. Time is money to the factory, and they won't sit around waiting. They will move on to something else and won't bother to call next time.

Check quality carefully. When you inspect production, compare everything against the standard set by your production sample. Measure the seams, test that the buttons and labels are secure, and check that the stitching is straight. Look for color consistency and for stains from the machine oil or glue. Inspect the pressing and packaging. Inspect a number of items again before you pay at the end of production and refuse to pay if they're not up to standard. If the factory can't get the quality right change factories.

If you choose to produce overseas you need a trusted agent or production manager to babysit production for you. Even if you have an agent or manager on location you still may need to visit yourself. Designers often move from Los Angeles to New York specifically to lessen the flight time to their production in Europe. Without proper oversight you can't ensure quality or even know if the factory is outsourcing the production to another company.

Designer Diego Binetti produces some of his womenswear line in China, and his business partner, Ada Lee, who is fluent in Chinese, travels to China for a month or more to oversee production each season. She is there to instruct the factory, explain the fit and stitching detail, and manage the quality every step of the way. If the factory in China makes mistakes that aren't caught before shipping, Diego has to use a factory in New York to fix everything. Being at the factory also led Ada to discover that the factory was using their pattern to make cheaper garments in different materials to sell as their own. This occasional shady practice can be stopped if someone is there to represent the designer.13

Producing in Italy has its own challenges and it's very hard to manage production and get things done on time. Flying to check on everything is not enough. Ideally, you need someone who is 100% on your side to be there all the time.

Menswear designer Douglas Mandel of Kamkyl says, "The most frustrating thing for him about producing in Italy is being constantly pushed back by bigger manufacturers, resulting in his jobs being late." Shoe designer Kristen Lee agrees, "You are pushed to the end for delivery and production from the tanneries, sole makers, last makers, heel suppliers, component suppliers, and dye-dip houses. Just one delay in the many components can cause a whole delivery to be late." She is now producing in Brazil where she found a production agent whom she trusts. She must oversee her production more now in terms of quality and has to be more specific with instruction. She visits Brazil once a season and then ships samples back and forth for review. She also has the new challenge of having less options for sourcing materials and must ship leather and hardware from Spain, Italy, and elsewhere.

Shoe production is complex and challenging and is why so many of the big brands license their shoe lines rather than produce them themselves. Shoe designers are experts on Italy because they spend significant time there. Most designers visit several times a year, even if they have a production agent located there. Also, attending the Linea Pelle leather show is key for meeting with the tanners, heel makers, and fit specialists. Holly Dunlap, designer of Hollywould shoes, moved to Florence. Michael Spaulding of Gunmetal shoes goes every month. He says, "In Italy, a little charm goes a long way. Drink their wine and tell them when it's the best prosciutto you've ever tasted. Then tell them you are not leaving until they finish your job."

Designer Alicia Bell manufactured some pieces overseas to save significantly on her production costs but when she received her shipment, along with the beautiful beaded pieces, there were endless problem. Stains and dirt on the garments, pen marks where the buttons were sewn on, buttons falling off, even a size 6 shirt with a size 12 sleeve on it! She had to spend many long days fixing the problem garments herself at her U.S. factory. Fortunately, she had an ironclad contract and didn't have to pay for the faulty production. Her attention to quality control and detail saved the collection.

There are ways to build relationships and find overseas factories to trust. Wendy Mullin of Built by Wendy recently moved some production to Shanghai. She knew the owners of the Shanghai factory from a factory in New York. They call her their American daughter and she knows her production is in great hands.

If you don't have someone to monitor production at the factory, have the factory send samples from multiple stages of the production run for your approval. Shipping will become a significant expense because of the constant back and forth but it's critical to guarantee good quality. Many Asian factories have very efficient and quick sample approval systems in place. Some visit New York each season to meet with their U.S. clients, review fabric and materials options, and even test first samples.

Other Costs Associated with International Business

Designers are often shocked when they receive the final fabric bill and discover the shipping and duty costs of bringing fabric into the country. When choosing fabric, find out whether the price includes shipping and insurance. Try to anticipate the total cost before you order. You don't want to end up like a menswear designer who had suiting from Italy sitting in customs for weeks as he tried to find the cash to pay unexpectedly high shipping and duty fees. His production was delayed each day his fabric sat in a port and U.S. Customs charged a daily storage fee for the goods.

Pricing terms specify which party covers the different costs of shipping. If the price is free on board (FOB), it includes only the transportation to the shipping port and not the shipping, duty, or other costs from that point on. Cost, insurance, freight (CIF) includes shipping but not duty.

To avoid surprises, ask for landed duty paid (LDP) where shipping and all duty is included in the quoted price. Many places won't ship fabric LDP leaving the difficult task of calculating duty to you.

A customs broker or freight forwarder can help accurately estimate the shipping and duty. Brokers are paid a percentage of your total order. Though expensive, UPS or DHL can be used for shipping small quantities under tight time frames. These companies will handle customs and it shouldn't take more than two or three days to receive fabric from Europe by air.

Shipping and Insurance

Sometimes fabric and garment manufacturing costs don't include shipping and insurance. It's important to factor those in. It's also important to factor in all the international shipping of pre-production garments, production samples, and other review items. This can add up very quickly.

Duties and Customs Fees

According to the Harmonized Duty Tariff Code, there is a different duty charge for each type of fabric and garment imported. Whereas linen might be charged 3%, the wool duty could be 30% radically affecting the total cost.

A designer who shipped 600 meters of white cotton from Italy that cost $1,100, had to pay $1,500 including shipping and duty which was an increase of about 36%. A fabric agent recently shipped fabric that was $7 a yard FOB but $13.50 per yard LDP. The duty charge almost doubled the price of the fabric. Duty is also affected by country of origin and the fabric's planned use.

Foreign Exchange Costs

Foreign exchange transactions each have a cost per transaction. It's important to factor those in and find ways to minimize these costs.

Licenses and Quotas

There may be additional import license costs for exotic leathers or other products. There are also applicable fees associated with importing garments and materials from overseas.

Question to Check

How much of a garment production is considered 'made in xx'? Some companies have tried going around various duties and quotas by having garments partially made elsewhere then shipping them and finishing the last steps in the US, so they are still considered made in the USA.

There are also particular countries to consider when manufacturing certain things. For example, sewing delicate and lightweight silk fabric items is better in China and Vietnam than in India while Indonesia has a lot of good cotton sourcing but no other fabrics.

2.9 Warehousing Costs

Costs that affect the wholesale price of a garment are warehousing and storage costs. Clothing warehouses provide storage for garments, fulfillment of orders and shipping to retailers and consumers.

2.10 Customs and Duties

Customs duties can significantly affect the wholesale price of a garment and the resulting retail price. It's important to keep in mind the following, to minimize duties.

Fabric Content

Some fabrics, depending on the protectionary measures of a country for a specific industry, are taxed more than others. And some garments with similar fabrics have different taxation rates. It's important to consider fabric content and taxation rates when choosing fabrics during the sampling stage. Substitute fabrics that have a lower duty if possible.

Country of Manufacturing

Depending on the country of manufacturing or place of production, there may be higher or lower tariffs or favorable rates.

2.11 Overhead and Operating Costs

Many designers forget to factor in the overhead for their product and to pay themselves a salary.

2.12 Salaries and Payroll for Staff and Designers

Salaries and payroll include pay for everyone working for the company as a full-time employee or contractor. This includes the accountant, office assistant, marketing and sales staff, graphic designer, assistant designer, and other people.

2.13   Office Expenses

Office, studio rental, utilities, and associated expenses.

2.14   Sales & Marketing Costs

Sales and marketing costs are important to include. These include external sales-associated costs like the showroom, trade shows, markets, and associated travel. It also includes the creation of sales materials, website maintenance, digital content creation, brand communication and PR.

2.15   Sales Rep and Showroom Costs

Showroom and sales rep costs are necessary for selling a brand. A designer should weigh the costs and benefits of an internal salesperson and an external showroom.

Advantages & Disadvantages of Selling Yourself as a Designer

One of the main advantages of a designer selling the line themselves is the first-hand experience and knowledge of getting the information and feedback straight from buyers. It's important for a designer to have some experience with the process and be able to sell a line. In most situations, designers are often the best spokespeople for their product and the most passionate.

Cost

Sales and product are two important areas where cutting costs can directly affect progress. A designer that tries to do everything is dangerous. A designer already must design, source, and oversee samples creation and orders production. Sales is a full-time endeavor and involves the constant research of stores, communication and follow-up.

An internal sales rep will cost between $32k - $50k per year plus a small commission percentage of around 2%. The more experience and established relationships they bring, the higher the salary. In addition, the designer must pay the full cost of trade show expenses and booth costs. Designers attending trade shows cannot share booths unless they're under the umbrella of a showroom that books the booth.

Advantages of Designers Doing the Selling

- Direct access to the feedback and to retailers and first-hand experience and knowledge of the product.

- Ability to establish and 'own' relationships with the retailers.

- Ability to react faster to retailer requests as opposed to having multiple parties involved in the communication.

Disadvantages of Designers Doing the Selling

- Designers need to establish a retailer contact list which takes time and effort. Showrooms and external reps generally have an established contact list.

- There are higher initial costs for a designer to do the sales than having a sales showroom. Paying $50k annually plus the cost of trade show expenses and paying $6k to $8k a year for a sales showroom and a fraction of the trade show and road expenses.

- If designers sell themselves, it costs the designer's time which could be used for other things.

Sometimes a designer must do the selling themselves for the initial seasons since many established showrooms will not take a new brand for the risk, time and energy that they represent. The larger the showroom, the higher the operating costs. Larger showrooms generally employ several full-time sales representatives, additional staff and are more stringent about their revenue potential expectations with the brands they work with.

Advantages and Disadvantages of Using a Sales Showroom

One of the main advantages of having external sales representation is the lower initial cost and their established retailer contact list. Having a sales showroom can help a designer by saving them time in establishing a retailer contact list and money on trade shows and road expenses that can be shared among a few lines. They also provide additional guidance and feedback for new brands.**Cost**

Depending on the city, a sales showroom will charge a showroom participation fee of $500 to $700 per month plus a commission of 10-14%.

The showroom participation fee is generally for a single location. There may be an additional fee for additional showroom locations. Larger showrooms will have additional locations in New York, Dallas, or other cities. The collection stays in a showroom permanently, which allows designers to have additional exposure from press, stylist, and buyers visiting the showroom.

Road representatives that don't have a showroom may charge a similar or lower monthly fee and an additional showroom fee during markets. In addition to the showroom costs, a portion of the tradeshow booth and travel costs are charged back to the designer.

Ultimately, the overall cost per year for a showroom and external sales is an additional $6K to $8k plus trade show expenses. This is nearly half the cost of a brand doing it themselves.

Advantages:

- An external sales showroom or representative has an established retailer contact list and can create a retailer target list for the brand.

- Existing retailer relationships.

- Lower monthly cost and dedicated effort focused on sales. Showrooms make money from commissions and have limited capacity for taking on new lines. It's in their interest to get orders and sell the lines they work with.

- Ability to share travel and trade show costs.

- Industry expertise and guidance. A good showroom can tell a designer what's going to sell and what will not be successful.

- Exposure to press, media, and additional opportunities.

- Better brand image. Being next to other established brands is good for a new brand and representation of a showroom creates a certain measure of confidence for retailers. They know a showroom is willing to take the risk of aligning themselves with that brand.

Disadvantages

- It's harder to control an external party than someone who is in-house. Showrooms work for other brands and may choose to focus their attention on brands that bring the highest revenue.

- Using an external sales rep may cost a less but you can cost more during markets as showroom and booth rental space for market for 3 to 5 days comes at a premium.

- There are many showrooms and representatives that are not a perfect fit for the brand. It will likely take several tries to find a good one. Some showrooms and reps take on new brands but spend less effort on them until they see retailer reactions. Other showrooms don't provide feedback or guidance to new designers on product development.

Designers should have a solid agreement in place that spells out what the showroom will be doing and the responsibilities of each party. Showroom agreements generally run 6 months to 1 year.

2.16   Sales and Marketing Materials

Sales and marketing materials are important for selling the product and communicating the brand vision. A lot of money is wasted on sales and marketing materials. Hundreds of dollars are spent photocopying line-sheets. Designers print thousands of look-books each season that are thrown out by retailers upon returning from a trade show or after the season has passed.

Ways to Save Money and the Environment

- Send orders digitally to minimize paper used. Email look-books and line-sheets with orders and create automated systems.

- Have postcards and foldouts that show enough of the line to give an idea. You may be able to spend more and have higher quality postcards than printing entire look-books.

- Print a limited number of look-books, give them only to chosen accounts, who ordered the line, not to everyone.

- Consider putting look-books and materials on CD's or memory sticks.

- Use cloud storage that people can easily access or password-protected websites.

Additional Marketing Materials

- Give away printed materials for the booth to remind people of the brand.

- Created branded items like t-shirts and bags.

2.17 Trade Show Costs

Trade show costs include booth costs, travel, shipping, entertainment and refreshments. Other trade-show associated costs are things like steamer rentals, additional fixtures and displays, hangers, mannequins, etc.

Ways to Control Trade Show Costs

- Sharing a booth with another brand or showroom.
- Picking only a few trade shows to attend and choosing road appointments over trade shows.
- Having people share a room at trade shows. If working the booth, using interns
- Negotiating with trade show account reps for a discount.

2.18 Marketing and PR Costs

This includes advertising costs, public relations, and any other event used for creating buzz.

Public relations costs include social media PR, PR showroom, fashion shows and fashion presentations, participation in other PR events like celebrity gifting suites, event sponsorship, etc.

PR and marketing costs also include garment giveaways to bloggers and celebrities in exchange for photos.

There are various ways to control PR and marketing costs. A brand should prioritize, define results, and know if the results are worth the costs involved for a clear return on sales.

General business ratios say that marketing costs should generally be a certain percentage of sales. Every industry has a different marketing to revenue ratio, including the fashion industry.

Overall Standards Across Different Industries

Utilize industry metrics to show where you stand in your sales and marketing costs as a percentage of revenue. Our recent survey of sales and marketing professionals and business leaders reported the following benchmarks.

2.19   Calculating Your Profit Margin

It's important for designers to calculate their profit margin. This is where a good accountant or bookkeeper can help.

Should there be a package of spreadsheets with formulas that can be sold to designers as a 'starter package' that then can be adjusted by a bookkeeper to help them track everything? This would be like the landed cost spreadsheet that Emblem created for all the overseas designers.

2.20   Profit Margin Guidelines

Research the profit margin guidelines for the fashion industry. It's important to look at the profit margin per garment and the overall profit margin per collection. In some situations, the lower profit margin on a garment may be offset by a higher profit margin on another garment.

2.21   Production Costs vs. Sampling Costs

In order to get started with production, you need to create or designate an approved sample to work with. This "sew by" sample, or design prototype, is the model the factory will use to create "bulk" production. If you are an apparel company, you will use these samples to define construction guidelines, fit specifications and the grading of sizes up and down.

When production is in process, it's important to monitor quality. Compare them to your samples that the buyers will use to write orders. The best way to do this is to visit the facility regularly. This is obviously easier when producing locally but don't underestimate the value travelling to see production before shipping.

Depending on the situation, you may be able to conduct fittings on test or bulk units to make sure they are executing correctly. If this is possible, it is highly advisable. If you are unable to visit your facilities, there are third party auditors that can oversee quality control for a fee.

2.22   How Sampling Costs are Allocate

Sampling costs include pattern making, sample making, and the sample materials.

Pattern Making

One of the first steps in producing a design is to create the patterns from which your samples will be made. It is critical to find good talent at this stage of production. A great patternmaker will pinpoint problems in the design, construction process, and materials. Exceptional pattern makers often reach celebrity status among designers.

Nicholas Caito, after gaining extensive experience at Lanvin and Rochas, was praised for bringing the technical craftsmanship of Milan and Paris to America. Elle magazine called him, "New York's most in-demand patternmaker." His fortunate clients include Peter Som, Proenza Schouler, and Hermes.

Designer Marni Joy said, "Finding a great patternmaker is one of the most important parts of the design process. I found someone early on whom I completely trusted and who did an amazing job. I left her because of cost, but I was back the following season realizing that it was worth the cost to avoid problems later on."

An expert pattern is the foundation of a good product. It determines fit, which is a common reason items don't sell. Signature items help put many designers on the map. Chaiken pant and the Shoshanna swimsuit are the results of a great pattern.

Who Should Make the Patterns?

You don't have to hire a patternmaker if you can do it yourself. Many new designers learn pattern making in design school. Some even teach themselves. Making your own patterns will save substantial money and give you control. It can help you interpret your design and manage alterations and turnaround time.

Have a clear conversation with the pattern maker. While communicating, be sure to listen to this person's advice and feedback. The pattern maker can suggest improvements and help you avoid problems in the design that will save money in production. Often new designers want a design in a fabric that just won't support the garment or fit correctly. A patternmaker can point this out up front before you waste time and money.

It's critical that you really have the skills to do an expert job or you will make mistakes and waste time and money fixing the production. Factory managers have told designers they won't work with self-made patterns anymore because the mistakes cause time delays at the factory. Even if you are extremely deft at patterns, they are time consuming and, as your company grows, you may have to outsource this task to focus on other aspects of the business.

If you don't make patterns, I highly advise you acquire a basic understanding of pattern making. The knowledge will help you better understand construction and fit, better communicate with pattern makers and other contractors, and be able to pinpoint and understand problems. A designer can be at the mercy of pattern makers if he doesn't speak the language. The patternmaker can blame problems with the pattern on the fabric or design and the designer won't know the difference.

Where to Find a Pattern Maker.

The best way to find a patternmaker is through personal referrals from people in the industry. However, designers are often protective of their best resources and will not always share. Ask contractors or factories if they can recommend someone. Contact the fashion schools and ask them to refer you to alumni in the field or even current students with strong pattern making skills.

If you know pattern makers who work for large companies, discreetly ask them if they do freelance work or if they know anyone who does. Keep in mind that this person has a full-time job and your work will come last.

Services, such as Infomat and Fashiondex, have websites, publications, and referral services to patternmakers and other contractors. Industry papers such as WWD and California Apparel News, often list pattern services in their classified sections. Don't be limited by geography since email and the

Internet make it possible to work with pattern makers from afar.

You get what you pay for. Good pattern makers are expensive, but money spent can save considerable money later. Most designers are willing to spend whatever is necessary for good patterns and will make their budget cutbacks elsewhere.

Generally, patternmakers charge by the piece and the complexity and amount of detail in the garment. Others charge an hourly rate and will provide an estimate of the number of hours required once they understand the garment. The more complex the pattern or garment is, the more time it takes and the more it will cost. Pricing can vary widely among different patternmakers and different areas of the country. Jackets fit into one price and range from $250 to $450, while skirt patterns usually cost less, from $100 to $200. Generally, the patternmaker will require a deposit before beginning work.

Confirm that the patternmaker will make revisions if you don't like the final sample. Revisions should be included in the price if something is wrong with the pattern but if you change the design based on the final sample, you will have to pay for the new pattern.

Communicate Clearly

Before the patternmaker can begin, the designer must know exactly how the finished garment should look, from the details of shape and fit to pocket placement. Both pattern makers and factories have stories of designers with ideas that are impossible to make. Designers are often frustrated when shown a sample that is nothing like what they envisioned.

Sketches of the front and back of the garment, technical drawings, and detailed specification sheets are valuable tools to communicate the measurements for the garment. Measurement including width of the pant leg at the hem and sewing details like the specific types of seams, spacing between pleats, size of pockets, special linings, and placement of trims.

Another option is to show the patternmaker a garment with similar attribute in a similar fabric. This will help explain what you want. One designer who works for a large fashion brand never bothers making patterns from scratch. Instead he goes to the Gap and buys a similar item to use as a starting pattern.

Sample Making First samples

The samples are the most critical tool for sales and require time and effort to perfect. Emerging designers spend as much as $80,000 for a single season's sample collection. Each sample can easily cost $1,000. Most young designers have a bad habit of oversampling. Keep your eye on the budget and limit the number of styles in the collection.

Who Should Make the Samples?

A designer does not need to sew. Many of the biggest names in the fashion business are lost in front of a sewing machine. While you aren't expected make your own garments, basic sewing skills are vital to understanding construction and fit and pinpointing problems with a sample that doesn't look right. Basic sewing skills help a designer communicate better with the factory and sample maker.

Making your own samples will save money and allow more control over the product and production schedule. Some new designers are extremely talented with a sewing machine and produce immaculate samples. IT's generally easy to spot samples made by a designer because they lack the quality and expert finish of a professional. Whether it's an issue of skill or just equipment, be honest with yourself. If your in-house samples aren't as good as they could be, outsource.

The same criteria you use for hiring a patternmaker applies to a sample maker. Inquire about expertise in the type of product you design. Review examples of past work and ask about turnaround time. Sample price is affected by the number of pattern pieces, the complexity of the garment, and the extra details of lining, topstitching, buttonholes, and finishing.

The factory you have found for production may offer sample-making services. If the factory makes the first sample, it will better understand the garment and be able to give you an accurate estimate of production lead time and cost. The cost of that first sample may be quite high. Sometimes, especially in New York, a factory will inflate the sample price considerably because of concerns that afterwards the designer will take the entire production to a cheap factory overseas. To counter this, the factory prices the sample high and then makes up for it in a cheaper production price as an incentive for the designer to keep the work there. Many overseas factories produce samples as part of their production package and then ship them to you for approval. Some even visit New York each season during the sample-making process to create samples or review them in person with the designer.

Be a Perfectionist

Terry Gillis, owner of the store TG-170 in New York, says, "When working with new designers, the biggest problem is usually the fit." A designer should do everything to ensure proper fit. Test each sample on a fit model who accurately represents the proportions of the target customer. The fit model will give movement to a garment and show whether it hangs correctly or if it pulls or sags. A model can also tell you about comfort and ease. Most likely, at least one round of alterations will be needed after trying the sample on the model. The sample should be redone until it's right.

Some designers act as their own fit model but with clothing, it's very difficult to get a full perspective of a garment on your own body and to pinpoint where it needs alteration. Before you finalize the collection, try the samples on a few real people to hear feedback and see how the samples hang on different bodies. I have seen shock on designer's faces when, after creating all their samples and perfecting them on a model, they realize how different the garment looks on a real body.

In addition to fit, check the sewing and construction details of the item. For clothing, do a wash test of the first sample to alert you to any shrinkage, fading, and stretching that result from care and cleaning.

2.23   Production Costs and Quantity Breakdowns

Fashion lives on a strictly set calendar with hard deadlines. For every collection, you'll need to master the production schedule. This includes each step of development from ordering fabric, first patterns, first samples, and sales. It also includes finalizing orders through the production processes of final patterns, cutting, sewing, and shipping. The schedule will track where each material is, at all times.

To create a schedule, start with the shipping dates and work backwards through all the steps. Schedule plenty of time for unexpected delays. Don't forget that the seasons overlap. At the same time that designers ship Fall orders, they are sampling for spring and may be producing holiday. Manage your time well.

Industry experts are quite serious when they recommend a designer design her first two or three collections before even starting her business since she will never again have the luxury of as much time to design. Production for your spring collection, which takes place in the fall and during the holidays, is much more crunched than production for fall, and the seasons overlap significantly.

Fabric selection often starts even earlier. When the European preview trade show takes place in June and July, sales may extend longer depending on the market. Menswear and accessories run on slightly different schedules. Menswear sells primarily in early July and January and ships in early January and August. Accessories have five markets per year that take place after the ready-to-wear markets. High-end accessories and shoe designers sell at the same time as ready-to-wear.

Production Schedules

Following a production schedule is very important. The fashion industry is cyclical, and schedule driven.

Here's the general schedule for sales, production, and sampling, for each season.

The First Cost Estimate.

Throughout the entire design and development process, it's important to keep track of every cost associated with the design and development of the first samples and be aware of how the costs of production will affect the final retail price. You don't want to create a product that no one can afford to buy.

The first sample will allow you to create the first production cost estimate for the item and verify that you can afford to produce and sell it at the appropriate price point. Designers roughly guess that the production cost for each item will be half the price of the sample. As you price out different quantities with suppliers and factories your estimate will become more accurate.

Production costs will change based on the orders you receive. The larger the orders, the less things cost due to volume discounts for materials and sewing. Small orders of each style can lead to production and material surcharges even if the overall sales figures are impressive. Wholesale pricing should be based on the costs of goods sold using quantity estimates.

Another reason to identify your production partner early in the process is because their execution capabilities and associated costs need to be figured into your early design decisions and your pricing. If you've followed our advice from earlier in this series, you should have already set wholesale and retail pricing targets for your product. By simple comparisons of these prices to your quoted costs, you should be able to tell whether they will allow you to make enough profit margin on each item at the right level of quality.

Many designers ask what a reasonable margin target should be. The answer, of course, varies depending on the size of your business, its overhead, development, sampling costs and many other factors. Most companies try to achieve close to 50% margins at wholesale and over 70% in retail. There are no hard and fast rules and each circumstance requires different treatment.

Remember that not all factories will have all the raw materials, fabrics, and trims required to construct your product. If procurement falls on your company, you will need to source these yourself. In doing so, you will incur costs that will likely need to be paid on an accelerated timeline. Most suppliers will require some sort of deposit or prepayment to cover raw materials and the labor needed for production. Whatever balance remains will usually be required once the goods are ready to ship.

Some suppliers will be flexible on terms and allow you to delay these payments for weeks to months. This will help your cash flow since you will not likely be paid by your accounts or customers for some time. Always ask for terms so you can give yourself some cushion on payments. Whatever arrangements you agree on with your suppliers should always be captured in an official purchase order that should detail all transactions and delivery terms.

The Costs of Production

Shoe production is extremely expensive because of the high cost of each component. Assuming you have a European factory to work with you, plan on the following costs for high-end shoe samples.

- Last (the solid form around which a shoe is molded) €75, each pair
- Heel €825, each pair
- Prototype €250, each style

This adds up to approximately €1,150 per pair, not including any special hardware or other features. To put a small collection of 20 styles together, using four lasts and three heels, would cost at least €7,775. It can easily cost more. One high-end shoe designer stated that just the model development of a collection of half-pair sales samples usually costs about $20,000 and does not include costs of new heels or lasts.

Shoe designers create two to four sample collections each year. Although the lasts can be reused, you will eventually need to add more as buyers want new shapes each season.

For the final collection, when the first samples are complete, edit the line to remove any samples that should not go to market. Some will need to be eliminated because they are too expensive, take too long to produce, or simply don't fit the collection. Once the line is finalized, make whatever duplicate samples are required for the selling process. You may need one set of samples for a New York showroom and one set to send to a West Coast sales representative.

Production Options

Production sources need to be lined up and ready before you begin to take orders. In fact, many designers recommend that you research and find your production options before you even start your company. Although there are alternatives, most designers choose to give their production to a factory or contractor.

2.24   Dealing with Production Minimums

Most suppliers of fabric and trim have a minimum amount of yardage (or meters in Europe) that designers can order. The minimums exist because for the supplier, servicing, shipping, and selling small quantities is less profitable. Each supplier has a different threshold of what quantities are worthwhile. Minimums can range from 15 to 5,000 yards. Generally, for the designer fabric market the average is around 300 yards. Certain fabrics from the same mill have different minimums, depending on the content of the fabric, the finishes, or the print.

When you are new to the market and your orders are small, meeting minimums can be difficult. New designers do not need, nor can they afford, to buy excess quantities of fabric. When approaching any source for fabric or trim, find out the minimums up front. Although this question will expose you as a little fish, possibly not worth the supplier's time, in my opinion, it's a waste of your time to discuss materials you can't have. You don't want to fall in love with a sample fabric that you can't get to produce your orders.

Not Meeting the Minimums

The reality is that new designers frequently cannot meet the minimums required by fabric suppliers but there are some things you can do.

Buy sample yardage. Generally, a supplier has two prices for fabric. One price for sample yardage, which is higher than a small amount of fabric that designers buy to create a test sample for the design. Another is the price for production yardage, which is a lower price charged for the larger quantities needed to produce store orders.

Sample yardage is expensive, 20% to 50% more than production yardage because the quantities are small. If you can't meet the required quantity for the production price, you can purchase the entire amount needed at the sample price. However, the cost will be high and there is a risk. It's possible the mill won't work with you next season because you didn't return for a larger production quantity.

Pay more. Sometimes a source will make a minimum exception if you pay more per yard or pay a fee. This is generally a much better deal than paying the full sample yardage price. Many European mills have expensive couture lines of fabric. Because the fabric is expensive, the profit margin is higher for the mill and it will sell that fabric in smaller quantities. You can also negotiate with the supplier to find other ways to get past minimums or keep your price down. Ask them if a major manufacturer is buying the fabric which will give you the opportunity to tag your order on to the end of the larger one.

Buy stocked fabric. Ask the mill or supplier what fabric it has in stock. Most places house a selection of fabrics that require smaller minimums. If they don't stock exactly what you want, such as black lace, they may have white lace you can dye. They may also stock greige goods that are unfinished and can be quickly dyed or treated.

Ask whether they sell off leftover fabric at the end of the season. If you do buy stocked fabric, find out how much they have in total. If they run out, you may be back to facing a 300-yard minimum to fill orders.

Be creative. Designers find other clever ways to deal with minimums. For example, if you offer a shirt in four colorways and the orders don't meet the minimums to buy the fabric in each color, you could buy the fabric for all of the shirts in white and dye it yourself.

Fabric Production Costs and Minimums

Factories also require minimums because small production runs are time consuming and less profitable. When reviewing a factory, find out its production minimum and try not to waste time with factories that are not an option for you. Many factories specialize in small lots or are at least open to negotiation, especially in New York and increasingly in Italy. More manufacturers are taking their production to Asia, forcing local factories to be more flexible and open to small companies.

Designers utilize several tricks to try to get around minimums. In a small industry, it's better to be straightforward and try to negotiate. If you don't meet the minimum, offer to pay more. For example, if the factory requires a 500-piece minimum at a price of $20 each, tell them you will pay $22 each for 250 pieces.

Realize if you negotiate this minimum up front and end up after market with orders for only 200 pieces, you must decide if you can take the loss on the extra 50 items or try to sell them elsewhere. In general, extra stock simply ties up your money and you will probably have some returns and extra inventory. Be very careful never to cut more than a 3% overage on your orders. If you can't sell enough to meet the factory minimum, it's best not to produce the piece at all.

Understand the definition of minimum. Some factories may have a minimum of 200 of each style, but that may include all sizes and several color options.

When negotiating, try to convince the factory owner that working with you now will lead to a large production run in the future. Ask about the production capacity of the factory to imply that you are planning to have big volume soon.

2.25   Sampling - Original Designs vs. Product Development

In some situations, it may be more cost and time-effective for a designer, especially a new designer, to use existing garments as basis for designs and illustration in conjunction with a sketch. Many chain stores and large retailers use it to facilitate sampling and production, especially when dealing with foreign factories, where interpretation of a sketch may be difficult.

In addition to an existing garment that may illustrate fit or styling lines, the designer needs to supply a technical sketch with all the details and measurements and a detailed description with instructions on how the garment will be different than the existing finished sample.

Straight-out copying is not ethical. It's considered stealing and called counterfeit. However, just as in music or books, there is a certain amount of similarity that may be acceptable. If a designer copies another designer, then what does that say about the brand the brand value?

Original Designs

Original designs often involve draping, many fittings, a muslin, and a pattern created from scratch. Depending on the time available and expertise of the designer and contractors, it may be more costly and time-intensive to create original designs and should be limited.

Product Development

Product development is also done by designers based on existing styles that are in their archives and modified to create new styles.

Advantages & Disadvantages of Each

- Save time and money from creating muslins and doing multiple fittings
- Start off with a fit or proven style that's considered good

2.26   Domestic vs. Offshore Production

The least glamorous, but possibly the most important aspect of bringing a fashion product or collection to market is production and manufacturing.

Production describes the process by which concepts are made into a saleable physical product. In most cases, this means going from a small set of samples or prototypes to commercial quantities of the item or style, often across multiple sizes, colors and patterns. As you can imagine, it's impossible to separate production from the overall success of a brand. Great concepts can be designed, developed and sold, but a fashion business will ultimately live or die based on what is produced and delivered to the end consumer.

For most small fashion brands and startups, finding sources of production is the most challenging element. Too often, early-stage businesses leave this until too late, and find themselves with orders to fulfil and no one to produce them. Avoid this at all cost. Once you have taken orders, you must be able to fulfil them or risk scaring away retailers for years to come.

While there are endless options for production, both domestic and international, finding quality suppliers can be difficult, especially in the UK and USA, where many top young fashion designers are based. As a result, many in the industry tend to be secretive and protective of their production sources.

2.27   Advantage and Disadvantages of Domestic Production

When starting out, it's highly advisable to produce domestically or even locally if possible. The ability to oversee each process and communicate directly with people at the factory will make it easier to keep production on schedule and meet quality standards. You also benefit from faster delivery to market and less danger of piracy which is a potential problem with overseas factories. It can also be easier to negotiate terms when you are meeting people in person. The downside is that domestic labor costs are high, and you may not find a factory with the expertise you need.

While most small designers in the United States produce in New York, there are production opportunities everywhere. California is the largest producer of apparel in the United States. Driving your production around in Los Angeles is easier than dragging it from block to block in New York. The Evans Group, with locations in Los Angeles and San Francisco, is a vertical company that specializes in contemporary and young-designer production with on-site pattern makers and sample makers.

There are designers in San Francisco, Dallas, Chicago, and Portland who produce in those cities and cite the advantages of working locally to produce specialized pieces, quick reorders, and small runs. Many smaller cities are working to support the local fashion industry by launching fashion weeks or creating programs that support designers.

For example, Mayor Richard M. Daley announced the City of Chicago's plans for the Chicago Fashion Incubator at Macy's on State Street. Is was an initiative to provide six emerging designers with mentoring on the business of fashion. Designers were offered sample production and showroom space at the State Street store. The incubator also provided workshops and seminars for the local fashion community.

2.28   Offshore Production

There is a wide variety of fabric to choose from overseas. European mills are known for high-end quality fabrics, such as Italian cashmeres, and innovative luxurious fabrics and prints. Japan has high-tech fabric. Korea has outerwear and synthetics. India has beading and silk and China offers a large variety of inexpensive goods.

Most designers work with at least some imported goods. Extra shipping and duty costs, shipping delays, customs, and vacation times are issues to consider when working with overseas sources. Italian mills are closed for the entire month of August. Asia has several holidays, some of which result in mills being closed for more than a week at a time. Long lead times can jeopardize delivery and the ability to fill reorders from the stores. For your first few seasons, buying overseas may not be worth the additional stress.

Advantages

- Cheaper labor and materials costs.
- More resources available and better fabrics.
- More experience and higher degree of specialization for some techniques.

Disadvantages

- Harder to manage overseas production.
- Additional costs
- Higher minimums

What to Watch Out For

Overseas production requires tight management, great communication, and good time-management.

2.29   Strategies for Managing Your Costs and Increasing Profits

Increasingly, factories and manufacturers have vertical operations and will source your raw materials for you. The factory can obtain discounts and demand quick and reliable delivery because it orders for multiple clients representing a large amount of business for the mill.

The designer may meet with the factory early in the development process to review options for fabric, trims, and even hardware such as zippers and buttons. Many overseas factories, such as the knitwear manufacturers in China, send packages of yarn options in various colors, fibers, and blends. For many designers, it is convenient to have choices laid out before them and know all the options are accessible. Then they don't have to worry about chasing the raw goods or taking up additional time shipping them from the supplier to the factory. Of course, the downside of this is that each factory has limited options. Many designers love the process of researching fabrics and sourcing each button as well as creating their own colors and prints.

2.30   Offshore Manufacturing

In many situations, it's cheaper to produce overseas. Even if there are higher quantities, because of the lower costs, it's possible to have lower retail prices that help sell higher unit volumes.

2.31   Product Development Short Cuts

There are some product development shortcuts and considerations that can help you manage costs and maintain profit margins.

Quality Control

The buck stops with you. You cannot accept bad work or compromise on quality. Quality control is critical at all stages of production right through to labeling and shipping. The buyers and the end customers have rules and expectations and if you don't meet their standards, the customers will return the product, stores will charge it back to you, and neither will give you another chance.

The store doesn't care if the factory made a mistake. It's your responsibility. Designer Nicole Miller describes her experience when all the beads popped off an entire shipment of sweaters for Saks Fifth Avenue. She had to eat the loss for the shipment because the store could not accept it and the factory was already paid with a letter of credit and could not be held liable.

Stay on Schedule

Delivery is key. If you are late, orders can be canceled and returned to you. Do everything possible to be on time or the stores might not work with you again. During production, try to anticipate delays. If you know that a shipment will be late, call the retailer immediately and ask for an extension and permission to ship. Find out if the store will accept a partial order on time and the rest later. If it won't accept that, you at least have some time to find another store that will.

Control Your Minimum Ordering Quantities

If you have high production minimums, it's important to be strict on the minimum order quantities that retailers must buy. Generally, if the goods are in-season and in-stock, the minimum order quantity may be less strict, allowing for designer to open new accounts. Minimum order quantity depends on the price level of garment and category...

Technology

A significant amount of software and technology are available to help apparel and accessories companies become more efficient throughout the entire process. There are systems that can collect data, plan better delivery cycles, manage costs and inventory, assist with patternmaking and fit, comply with electronic data interchange (EDI) and other department store requirements, track samples, and more.

Most technology investments are extremely expensive and should not be a priority for small companies. They should preserve capital until they build up enough volume to warrant making these investments. You should first concentrate on growing your sales volume and shipping on time. Then slowly add infrastructure to your business.

COO of Loeffler Randall Amanda Thomas's advises design entrepreneurs to get a good computer education in Excel and other software, as you will spend much time on the computer organizing, planning, scheduling, and analyzing.

Most early-stage designers rely on Excel to handle most of their needs. For costing, you can design a spreadsheet to track all your expenses and calculate the total cost, wholesale price, and profit margin for each collection.

Excel is also good for creating and managing production schedules, working backwards from your delivery dates through each stage of production and raw materials sourcing. It can generate business reports, such as sales by city and state, sales by size and color, this season's profit versus previous seasons. The reports will help you analyze the best and worst markets and styles and help you create a plan for next season.

For accounting, most early-stage designers rely on QuickBooks. If your business scales up significantly, you may need more sophisticated financial software.

Once you start to research other technology, the place to start is with an Internet-based software system that will work with your existing Microsoft or other operating system and allow you to avoid making any significant hardware investments.

Internet-based systems are ideal for helping you communicate more efficiently with factories and suppliers. For example, sending a multi-page paper fax to India with the unreliable phone lines and frequent disconnections can lead to delays in production, mistakes in communication, and waste time following up and resending information.

With a web-based system, you create a central repository for all your schedules, inventory, and production requirements and communicate in real time with mills, factories, customers, sales, and warehousing. A web-based system enables all parties to access and work off the same accurate and up-to-date information using a secure user ID and password. Some Internet-based solutions make it easy to share visuals with your suppliers and vendors, illustrating communications regarding materials, samples, and production.

In general, the key efficiencies that a designer should seek are applications that integrate order entry, production planning, and financial operations. This will save significant time on administrative activities. For example, enterprise resource planning (ERP) and merchandising software, such as LogOns small business solutions, help track information across all sizes and styles to help with the sales cycle, production planning and management, inventory management, and financial accounting. Also, some Web-based programs help with sales order processing, customer relationship management (CRM), and even e-commerce issues such as online shopping carts.

A good software will create reports on what has and has not been shipped. It will also tell you what supplies have been delivered when and where, returns, factor reports, accounting and tax reports, customer management and communications, contact and mailing lists, commissions to salespeople or showrooms, retail discounts, markup and profit margins, duty tracking, invoice and packing slip creation, as well as inventory management issues, such as styles by color, size, and style number; season; price; fabric content; delivery date; inventory allocation to orders; the percentage of stock that sold at full price versus on mark-down; comparing forecasts to actual sales; and building new forecasts based on past trends.

Supply chain management (SCM) technology is generally the most sophisticated option available to plan the flow of goods and information. Starting with raw materials sourcing through production, shipping and final delivery and reorder. It can organize and automate communication and scheduling throughout the design and production chain and help you analyze the efficiency of the entire operation versus just each part.

For example, China may be the cheapest place to produce but if it takes an extra week to get the goods from China it may be worth the extra cost of production to get the goods earlier and onto the floor selling at full price. A truly efficient supply chain will shorten lead times, ensure on-time delivery, raise productivity, reduce costs, and minimize inventory by helping the designer produce what has been sold rather than selling what has been produced.

Design software is another key area of interest for early-stage companies. It lets designers create their collections and store all styles and materials in the application's memory to make easy updates and modifications in color, design, or fabric. These programs can help you create specs and draw flats. Some even include fit applications and three-dimensional models in a broad range of colors and materials. They can also help you review collections, reduce the number of actual samples required, and communicate in visual detail with the factory.

Ordering Production Materials

Wait until you have responses from buyers before ordering production materials. Although large companies make sales predictions and order their fabric and trims in advance, small companies should cut to order. This means only producing exactly what is necessary to ship. The mills do not accept returns and if fabric is ordered in advance and the style doesn't sell, the designer will be left with it.

Some new designers overstock in hopes of reorders but quickly learn that it wastes money. However, if some of your fabric is from overseas and has a long lead time, you may need to order the production yardage before sales are finalized to stay on schedule. In this case, wait as long as you can and work closely with the salespeople to get accurate quantity projections.

Clearly order the correct fabric using a swatch. Confirm the delivery lead time, cost, and shipping information. Know how much yardage it takes to produce each piece and don't buy too much. A very small amount of excess can cover damaged or unusable goods, but too much stock will go unused and eat up your profit margin.

Track the Production Materials

Create a system or chart to keep track of every material needed for production and where it is in the ordering process. The chart should include everything required for the item from fabric, lining, thread, and interfacing to buttons and zippers.

Do everything you can to ensure all materials arrive at the factory on time and in the right quantities to avoid scheduling problems at the factory. Most factories won't start a job until all the components are there. They don't want to risk setting up all their machines with your green thread only to discover the zippers aren't arriving for three more days. If the fabric or other materials will be late, tell the factory manager immediately so he or she can plan to fit your job in later.

2.32   Re-using and Modifying Existing Bodies to Save Development Costs

Reusing and modifying existing bodies is a way to save costs in sampling and production.

Varying Fabrics and Trim

Cutting the same silhouettes in different colors and fabric combinations and incorporating different trims will save money on patterns and production and help meet minimums. Even though the garments look like different styles, for production, the cutting and sewing steps are the same and you will be charged a lower price as if it is the same garment. Observe collections in the stores to see the smart ways that designers save money on fabric and production. At the Rebecca Taylor store, for instance, a tuxedo pant is offered in several different colors of wool, and the same silhouette is available in satin and with varying trims.

Varying Length to Create New Styles

Using the same body and just varying the length can turn a dress into a top or a top into a dress with minimal changes.

Control the Number of Fabrics Used in the Collection to Reach Minimums

Controlling the number of fabrics used in a collection will help you reach minimums for production. Depending on the minimum, you can also use one fabric with a high minimum for a lot of styles and add a different fabric that may be less minimum and in stock, to add interest.

Vendors with In-Stock Fabric

Use in-stock fabrics if possible and vary between basic fabrics and novelty fabrics.

Consider Garment Dying Option

If doing basics that stay the same across different seasons, consider garment or fabric dying. This could work for jersey t-shirts or other pieces that are easy to dye.

Small Runs from Fabric Remnants a Sustainable Practice

If possible, limit production to small runs for certain fabrics. Then you can use fabric remnants from jobbers. That can work if you have some basic core styles and you're re-issuing them every few months in different colors.

2.33   Balance Your Profit Margin Across the Line and Collection

It's important to look at the profit margin per garment and for the entire collection. In some situations, a lower profit margin on a garment can be offset by a higher profit margin on another garment.

However, if a designer has to make a lower profit margin in order to be a leading store that's considered an influencer, it might make sense for the designer to produce the order. Some people believe it's important for new designers to produce all their orders, regardless of size.

Research what should be the profit margin guidelines for the fashion industry.

Develop Some Styles that Give You a High Profit Margin

It's important to create some 'cash cow' styles that season after season provide a lot of revenue and are very profitable.

It might make sense to have a few styles that are less profitable but good for the brand's overall image. Furthermore, it's important to define minimum order quantities for retail buyers.

2.34 Develop Relationships with Garment Manufacturers and Contractors

In recent years, producers in France and Italy have become more open to working with young designers. However, orders in small, unpredictable quantities tend to get pushed to the back of the order queue. Your deliveries may be later than bigger brands and have negative impact sell-through rates and vendor relationships.

With so much competition for vendors, it's essential to make sure you can secure production before you invest time and money in the design process, sales process and marketing costs.

So how can you track down production resources? As with most things in fashion, it comes down to leveraging your relationships and seeking out help wherever you can find it.

Former Partners: If you've worked for another company previously, especially a larger one, some of your former producers may be willing to work with you or at least make a referral.

Accounts: Often a retailer will have preferred production partners that their other accounts work with. They may even use them for their own private label product and be willing to make some introductions.

Sample Makers: Many small manufacturing labs or factories who create samples often have associated production facilities or know the best local manufacturers. Use them as a resource as they may be able to point you in the right direction.

Fashion Schools: If you are a student or alumnus of a fashion school, check in with your professors and tutors to see what resources are available to you. They may have relationships you can leverage.

Friends and Colleagues: It never hurts to ask but you may not get a straight answer.

Online Resources: There are some very helpful sites that, for a fee, will give ratings and testimonials on apparel and textile manufacturers. Panjiva.com is a great example. You may be hard-pressed to find top-quality resources if you operate at the luxury end of the business.

Convincing Suppliers to Work with You

Mills and fabric agents are often hesitant to work with new designers. A designer told me she approached a supplier who was standing in front of a rack of black ribbon, and when she asked, "Do you have any black ribbon?" the supplier said no.

The relationships you develop over time with fabric, leather, and trim suppliers will be invaluable. Fabric Company CEO Wen Zhou put up $750,000 from her business for designer Philip Lim to start his label. It's not surprising that designers who speak fluent French or Italian often evade the minimums at European mills. A supplier of active wear fabrics at the IFFE told me that even though he has a 500-yard production minimum, if he enjoys speaking to a young designer and determines from the conversation that the designer is serious and smart, he may let that person buy small quantities with a credit card.

Some fabric suppliers enthusiastically support new designers. Erich Soldat of Textile Agency said, "Young designers bring energy and creativity to fashion and keep New York fashion from being boring." Jasco Fabrics supports new talent and allows new designers to order small quantities of its high-quality, American-made jersey.

To increase the odds of getting fabric from a new supplier, introduce yourself, demonstrate some knowledge of fabric, share your vision, and mention interest in your collection from press or stores. Let the supplier see the potential for increased business and convince them you can pay.

If a rep does give you an appointment, be prepared and don't waste the rep's time. Agent Erich Soldat emphasizes, "No designing here!" If you start developing your concept in a supplier's office while looking at all the fabrics and asking for random swatches, you won't be invited back. Have your concept and direction for the collection before you meet the fabric agent. Tell the agent exactly what you need so she can help you find it quickly.

Sourcing fabric will get easier. Ingwa Melero's fabric suppliers now stock some of its fabrics to help with reorders and they bring previews of upcoming fabrics to see if the designers want special colors or details.

Attend Sourcing and Fabric Shows on a Regular Basis

It's important to attend sourcing shows to see new fabrics, meet new manufacturers, and order sample yardage.

Keep Adding to a Contact List

It's always important to keep a good contact list with notes on who has what fabric and maintain contact with suppliers. Sometimes by staying in touch with them you may get advance notice of new fabrics and insider knowledge.

Get Referrals and Samples of Work

Production sources need to be lined up and ready before you begin to take orders. Many designers recommend that you research and find your production options before you even start your company. Although there are alternatives, most designers choose to give their production to a factory or contractor.

Not Everyone Wants to Work with You

Like the fabric suppliers, factory owners often feel that new designers are not worth the extra work. New designers have more problems, pattern mistakes, materials that aren't appropriate for the product, incorrect cutting, and other issues that take time to organize and fix. For a factory, time is money.

Factories often require references, especially overseas. Micheal Spaulding of Gunmetal says, "You can't just walk into a factory in Italy and have them work with you. A last factory won't even give you an appointment without a recommendation from someone in the industry."

Factories are concerned about your credibility and whether you can pay. They will ask about your business history and the projected production run.

Referrals to Factories and Contractors

Finding and reviewing factories is time consuming and can be frustrating. Ideally, you will receive recommendations from designers or others in the industry. Fabric shows are also a good source of information. In general, you just need to ask around.

For example, if you are making leggings, ask the supplier of the stretch fabric and which factory could sew them. Panjiva is a New York based company that helps fashion brands find and evaluate factories with a database of more than 40,000 apparel suppliers around the globe. The chambers of commerce of Italy, China, Hong Kong, and India can help you find factories in those countries.

Don't disregard the importance of the garment industry's old boys 'club. The factory owners know everyone and will refer you to other contractors, suppliers, and a wide range of specialists. There are ads for contractors in trade papers, and referrals are available at the Fashion Information Center and the Garment Industry Development Corporation in New York, as well as the Garment Contractors Association in Los Angeles. Infomat and Fashiondex have resources online and in their books. While these sources will provide long lists of potential options, you will need to research and knock on doors to find the place that is right for you.

2.35   Costing Do's and Don'ts

Here are some things to consider with costing.

Do

Track all costs but don't be penny-wise and pound foolish.

Sometimes efforts to save are short-sighted. Someone may save a few pennies here but short-change themselves later. See how much you can save and the potential problems you may encounter.

Assume a 15% to 20% "fudge factor" when budgeting.

It's good if you can add a margin of error to your calculations and costs. There are always unforeseen circumstances and it's good to have a little extra room.

Find creative, cost-cutting solutions that don't hurt the quality of your product

It's important to be clever when cutting costs and to have an open mind. It's also important to understand what the perception is for the product. If cutting costs creates the perception that the product will be lower quality, consider doing something different altogether.

2.36   Don'ts and Common Mistakes

Wait too long to buy fabric.

Sometimes if you wait too long to buy fabric, there might not be enough lead time.

Have too many fabrics in the collection

It's important to manage the number of fabrics in the collection. This varies with the number of groups and size of the collection.

2.36   Shipping and Delivery

When goods are ready and approved to be released, you will likely have them shipped or delivered. Some companies will "drop ship" directly to their own retail stores or accounts. Most often, the goods are received in an office or distribution warehouse. Once you take possession of the final products, you should make sure to pull some or all the units to check for quality on execution. This extra time and money is well spent considering that your customer or account is likely to return any faulty or ill-fitting product. Remember to have a clear understanding of any packing parameters required by specific accounts. Failure to adhere to these parameters can result in charge backs and even order cancellations.

All in all, production can be the most complicated and cumbersome part of running a fashion business. If you have the resources to hire an experienced production manager, they will often be able to bring both know-how and sourcing contacts to your company. A production specialist is often one of the first hires a growing brand will make. Those of you still considering a career direction in fashion who have a mind for managing complex processes and logistics and an eye for product, should keep this in mind as it is consistently one of the most in-demand skills in the fashion industry.

2.37   Replacing the Goods

Sometimes, you may need to replace fabric or supplies even after you have shown your samples and taken orders. The jobber may run out of the goods or the fabric may arrive too flawed to use.

When replacing materials, try to match the original as closely as possible in terms of quality, look, and feel. Once you find something, you should show it to the buyers who ordered the affected items for approval. There is a risk that they won't approve the replacement or will use the change as an excuse to cancel the order. It's still better to deal with this at this stage than later when the items are already produced and shipped. A menswear designer told me that he doesn't ask buyers if the replacement is close enough because they placed the order six months ago and won't remember exactly what it looked like. However, if they do remember, they could return the entire production.

When you replace goods, make sure the production bundles don't mix the original fabric with the replacement or you may deliver a garment with one fabric on the body and another on the sleeves. Remember to include any cost differences resulting from replacement materials on the cost sheet.

If you went to fashion school, you probably learned about the production process as it relates to big companies. It is very challenging to navigate the world of production on your own. Many designers name production as the part of their job that is the most difficult and some even say it's the only part they hate. Despite the frustration, production is where your brilliant ideas become reality.

A critical person in large fashion houses is the production manager. For most new designers this will be you. The designer must manage all the steps of production from initial samples through final shipping. They must plan carefully to stay on schedule, meet retail delivery dates, and keep track of every cost from start to finish. Don't take anything for granted, actively oversee it all.

2.38   Production Management

Once you have taken the collection through the sales process and confirmed the orders, you will know which items will be produced, in what quantities, and with what required delivery dates. Now it's time to start production.

The production process is extremely critical and time consuming. Between constant problems and a tight schedule, it requires someone to manage each stage of the process, from dealing with raw material deliveries to final shipping and quality control. Whether you are fortunate enough to have a production manager or are attentively filling the role yourself, careful production management is critical to ensuring quality

2.39 Packing and Shipping

At most small companies, the designers and their staff personally pack and ship the goods. On the bright side, it's an ideal time to interact with each product and check that quality standards have been met. The designer can control the packing process and make sure that directions from the stores are carefully followed.

Retailers, and in particular department stores, have specific packing and shipping instructions that must be followed, or the store will refuse the goods or issue chargeback fees.

Read the routing guide from the store thoroughly and follow the directions. Packing details cover whether the garments should be on hangers or packed flat in bags, wrapped in plastic, or tagged in a specific place with specific information. Shipping instructions indicate the shipping method that should be used, the documentation and packing slips required, and the format for labeling the boxes. Don't forget to order packing materials in advance. While some of these requirements seem overly demanding, realize that the stores receive thousands of items each day.

To get your goods onto the selling floor quickly, the box labels, packing slips, packing bags, and hangtags must provide all the information to help the stores quickly process the boxes and items. They should be able to tell the style, name, number, size, color, and even the neckline style or sleeve-length without unpacking or unfolding each item.

Take your time and pull each order one at a time. Confirm whether the shipment is insured by the shipper or the retailer. Once shipped, track the deliveries. When shipping small amounts overseas, FedEx, DHL, or UPS can act as a customs broker. Once you start shipping in volume, it's preferable to use a freight forwarder or fulfillment service that can help with paperwork and international shipping regulations, book the shipping, arrange for insurance, and save money through consolidation.

2.40   Fulfillment Centers

At some point, you will want to work with a fulfillment center rather than handle all the tagging, shipping, and packaging of product in your own studio. As your volume grows, shipping becomes too time consuming and complicated and takes up too much space. When selling to department stores, it can be critical to work with a fulfillment center to meet all the vendor compliance requirements correctly and avoid chargebacks and returns. Shoe label Loeffler Randall, which produces shoes in Italy, bags in Korea, and apparel in New York, now works with a fulfillment center.

Amanda Thomas, named growing pains in shipping as their biggest current challenge. With only a 15 to 20-day window, they need to coordinate items coming from all over the world to be packaged together in mixed orders for multiple accounts.

Fulfillment centers offer a range of services and capabilities and you can negotiate a package based on your business needs. They will charge you for storage and shipping according to your selections from a menu of other services.

A fulfillment center may offer warehousing and inventory management, garment on hanger (GOH) shipping, pick order or batch order processing (assembling mixed orders of items that arrive from different manufacturers for shipping to multiple customers), processing returns, customs clearance, hang tag and price ticket application, credit checks, invoicing, and a range of barcode and EDI-compliant services.

Electronic data interchange (EDI) is the electronic exchange of information between two computers. Most department stores require vendors to be EDI-compliant and to use barcode technology on their shipments. Department stores receive thousands of items each week and need to organize and process them quickly to get the goods onto the selling floor. EDI and barcode technology, used to label boxes and individual hang tags on the items, enable this process.

It is generally too expensive for a newer designer to invest in this technology, so you should ask for an exemption from a department store for at least the first few seasons. If a fulfillment center has the EDI and barcode software, you will be able to comply earlier without making the investment yourself. As a result, the stores will get your goods onto the floor more quickly, allowing them more time to sell at full price and you will avoid the expensive charge backs that result from packing and shipping errors.

Many fulfillment companies have a minimum, so you need to make sure you have the orders to meet the requirements. Make sure your fulfillment company has insurance and that it is EDI-compliant and can meet the requirements of your department store clients. Ask what discounts it has with the major shipping companies, such as UPS and FedEx, how fast it can turn around orders and ship, and if it offers same day shipping.

3. PRODUCTON MANAGEMENT AND STRATEGIES

3.1   Production is the Key to Revenue and Profits

Production is just as important as design. The production process makes it possible for designs to be turned into product and delivered to buyers so the designer can be paid. It's virtually impossible to separate production from the overall success of a brand. Great concepts can be designed, developed and sold, but a designer's success is ultimately based on what is produced and delivered to the end consumer. Without production there is no revenue or profits.

If you went to fashion school, you probably learned about the production process as it relates to big companies. It's challenging to navigate the world of production on your own. Even the most experienced production managers find new challenges and problems with many of their orders. Many designers cite production as the part of their job that is the most difficult.

Production management applies to all orders in the fashion business, irrespective of the size. The same pressures, problems and delays will affect you, whether you are making 50 garments or 50,000 garments a season. The only difference between those two scenarios are the numbers.

A critical person in large fashion houses is the production manager. For most new designers, this means you. The designer must manage all the steps of production, from initial samples through final shipping. They must plan carefully to stay on schedule, meet retail delivery dates, and keep track of every cost from start to finish. Don't take anything for granted but actively oversee everything.

A production specialist is often one of the first hires for a growing brand. Production specialists consult with designers at specific points in the product development process to ensure production is well managed and may have additional production factories or resources to refer to designers.

The relationship between the designer and the manufacturer can be challenging and it's important for each side to understand the basic requirements. Designers need to build good working relationships with their factories and remember that factories are businesses that rely on smooth and constant production to create profits.

3.2   Designing with Production in Mind

It's sometimes easy for a designer to view production as separate from design, especially when samples are made in-house or by someone outside of production. Designers should remember that what they sample and sell (take orders for), must be produced. Samples must be easy to produce by a factory with fabrics and notions that are available and easy to source.

As fabrics and trim are chosen for samples, consider if they are realistic for production and the potential production costs. If there's manual work needed in production like hand-beading, hand-assembly of fabric flowers or other trim, consider how it will affect labor costs and the overall cost of production. If the styles are important for creating PR buzz for the line, they should be priced accordingly with a conscious decision about their production feasibility and quantities.

3.3 Production Issues to Consider During Design

When designs are created for a line, the following production considerations must be addressed as they affect the cost of goods (COGS).

a) **Sourcing of Materials:** Are these materials available in larger quantities and are they easy to source?

b) **Timelines:** Is there a delay for producing the materials in addition to cutting and sewing the garments? Is additional time needed for prints? What's the latest date that production can start to meet the ship date?

c) **Minimums:** Are there production minimums for fabric and materials?

d) **Production Price & Minimums:** Is there a minimum quantity for producing each style (cutting, sewing, finishing)? What are the quantity and price breakdowns?

e) **Special Techniques or Equipment:** Are there special techniques or equipment that are needed to produce the garments? Does the factory have the necessary resources to do this or will a separate contractor be needed?

f) **Ease of Production:** Are the garments easy to produce? If there was a lot of manual adjusting in the sample-creation phase, it may be necessary to make minor adjustments for easier production.

g) **Prints:** Print direction may complicate production. Placement prints will require additional accuracy.

There may be other considerations for designs that will affect production. For this reason, work with experienced sample makers and pattern makers or start by modifying existing patterns and styles that have already been produced.

3.4 Manage Costs, Schedules, and Quality for Successful Production

Whereas, the design phase in the lifecycle of a product is characterized by creativity and innovation, the production phase is characterized by process, structure, and discipline. For production to be successful, it's important to manage costs to ensure profit margin, schedules and timelines to ensure deadlines are met, and quality to ensure product requirements are met.

A survey that asked designers which employee was the most important to hire, many reported the production manager. Whether you are fortunate enough to have a production manager or you are like most start-up designers and are filling the role yourself, careful production management is critical to ensuring quality and timely delivery.

3.5 Cost Management

Once you have taken the collection through the sales process and confirmed orders and know which items will be produced, in what quantities, and the required delivery dates, it's time to start production.

Cost sheet analysis is essential for determining which products will be profitable. The cost sheets must take include fabrics, trims and findings, marking and grading, cutting, sewing, finishing, labels, tags, and shipping.

Fabric Cost Management

Fabric is an important, visible input for a garment.

Material costs are a factor of cost per yard multiplied by fabric usage. The choice of fabric or trim in the design and development process affects the price per yard/meter. Other factors to consider in calculating material cost for fabric are the size of the markers vs. the width and length of the fabric (larger sizes need more fabric), fabric placement and fabric allowances. A standard average of 10-15% for fabric loss should be included.

Replacement of the Fabric

At times, you may need to replace fabric or supplies even after you have shown your samples and taken orders. The jobber may run out of the goods or the fabric may arrive too flawed to use.

When replacing materials, try to match the original as closely as possible in terms of quality, look, and feel. Upon finding a replacement, show it to the buyers who ordered the affected items for approval. There is always a chance the buyers won't approve the replacement or will use the change as an excuse to cancel the order, but it better that cancellations happen at this stage rather than later, when items are already produced and shipped.

A menswear designer once told me he doesn't ask buyers if the replacement is close enough because after placing the order six months ago, they likely won't remember exactly what it looked like even though they could return the entire production if they do remember.

When you replace goods, make sure the production bundles don't mix the original fabric with the replacement to prevent delivering a garment with one fabric on the body and another on the sleeves. Include any cost differences incurred from replacement materials on the cost sheet.

Marker Planning to Reduce Fabric

Marker planning is very important in assessing the cost of fabric. Marker planning can be viewed either as the first operation in the manufacturing process or as an operation in the design and development process. This is the first point in which all pattern pieces are studied together inside the rectangle of a marker and in relation to the fabric from which the garment parts will be cut.

In order to make decisions about the commercial profitability of a style, the marker maker must have a preliminary estimate for the design and product development process.

Factors that are considered with pattern marking include pattern grain alignment, pattern facing (all pattern pieces should point in the same direction for one-way fabric), vertical stripes and checks.

Some questions to ask when assessing the cost of fabric include:

- Is there a similar fabric that I can substitute at a lower cost that will look the same?

- Can I use a lower-priced fabric for facing or lining?

- What fiber content is important for the fabric? Can I use fabric blends instead of all-natural fiber?

Ordering of Production Materials

Wait as long as you can before ordering materials, but ensure you have enough time to produce the fabric. Large companies make sales predictions and order their fabric and trims in advance. Small companies should cut to order, or produce only what they know they will sell, and make accurate projections. If fabric is ordered in advance, mills don't take returns, and it's important for the designer not to be stuck with extra fabric. If the fabric is from overseas and has a long lead time, you may need to order the production yardage before sales are finalized to stay on schedule. If there might be extra fabric, it's important for the designer to consider the ways that fabric will be used in the future or sell it to a jobber (for cents on the dollar) to recoup some costs. A very small amount of excess can cover damaged or unusable goods, but too much stock will go unused and eat up your profit margin.

Clearly order the correct fabric using a swatch. Confirm the delivery lead time, cost, and shipping information.

Tracking the Production Materials

Create a system or chart to keep track of every material needed for production and where it is in the ordering process. The chart should include everything required for the item such as fabric, lining, thread, interfacing, buttons and zippers.

Do everything you can to ensure all materials arrive at the factory on time and in the right quantities to avoid scheduling problems at the factory. Most factories won't start a job until all the components are there. They won't risk setting all of their machines with your green thread only to discover that the zippers aren't arriving for three more days. If the fabric or other materials will be late, tell the factory manager immediately so he can plan and make arrangements to fit your job in later.

If using a vertically integrated production facility that sources the materials themselves, there is normally an internal person who track all of the materials throughout the production process.

Trim & Findings Cost Management

When considering trim and findings, cost management is necessary to assess profitability. The following factors should be considered:

a) Are there similar buttons or findings at a lower cost that could be used?

b) For buttons, can the cost be lowered by reducing the number of buttons or using another closure?

c) If offering the garment in different colors, it may be necessary to source trim and findings in matching colors. Are there minimums for each color? Are colors available? If it's trim, can it be dyed?

d) Would it be cheaper to use self-covered buttons? Is there a labor cost associated with covering buttons?

e) If there are minimums, can these buttons be used in another style?

Pattern Grading & Engineering for Cost Savings

Grading the pattern for the different sizes happens at production. To reduce unnecessary grading costs, designers should consider what sizing is most appropriate, either letters (XS-XL) or numbered sizes (0-12). If the garment is fitted and there is no stretch, numbered sizes are appropriate. If the garment is more sportswear and looser fitting, use letter sizes.

Reviewing the pattern for fabric and labor savings opportunities can include removing unnecessary seams, adjusting pieces for easier manufacturing and dividing large, awkwardly shaped patterns into two pieces, to accommodate the marker if it's possible and cheaper than sewing 2 pieces together.

Cost Management for Sewing & Cutting

It's important to explore all cost-cutting practices at every level of production. Generally, sewing and cutting costs depend on the number of pieces produced so you will want to have production breakdowns for discounts.

Some things to consider are:

a) If you are close to the minimum units for a production discount, it's worth the time to calculate the overall savings gained per product with a higher quantity and see if you can sell additional pieces.

b) If using a separate cutter and sewer, check the minimum quantities for cutters

c) Does the factory have the necessary capacity to produce the units in the least amount of time you need them in order to ship?

3.6 Time & Schedules Management

The production process is extremely critical and time consuming. Constant problems and tight schedules require someone to manage each stage of the process, from dealing with raw material deliveries to final shipping and quality control. Garment production is like a football game. There are many moving players and a quarterback, the production manager, whose job it is to complete production within the allotted time while leading a team people with different skill sets.

Delivery is key. If you are late, orders can be canceled and returned to you. Do everything possible to be on time or store won't work with you again. During production, anticipate delays. If you know that a shipment will be late, call the retailer immediately and ask for an extension. Find out if the store will accept a partial order on time and a second delivery later. If they don't accept an extension you will at least have some time to find another store.

Tracking Information: Sales Orders and Production Orders

This is the first stage in the manufacturing process. Without creating an overview of your production requirements, you will tackle the manufacturing process in a piecemeal fashion with disastrous consequences.

Collate all Purchase Orders to Order Fabric & Trim

Once you have taken orders and now the total number for each style, you need to calculate the requirements for every fabric, button, zip and label and get them ordered as soon as possible. It is vital to obtain a clear delivery date from your fabric and trim suppliers. You should have a rough idea of these times to be sure you are not quoting unrealistic ship dates to your buyers.

The factory will usually base their delivery to you on the date that you can give them the complete set of components that they will need to create the order. The factory cannot quote an accurate date unless they have all the fabric and trim information. Many orders are delayed each season because something is not supplied on time. Track the delivery dates of your fabric and trim on your production schedule.

Production Schedule

If you don't have a production management system, you can create a production schedule spreadsheet that shows the total number of orders against each style and the applicable delivery details. This schedule will form the foundation of your production management system.

There must be a production schedule with dates for all stages of production and styles. The schedule must include dates for the fabric ordering deadline, fabric deliveries to the factory, start and end of production, start shipment, and the complete shipment.

A production manager will need to track the schedules and arrivals for all the fabrics and trim. If producing domestically, this function must be ensured by the designer or the designer's factory. If there are any delays in production schedules, the delays must be communicated in a timely manner to the retailer.

Regardless if the production is done overseas, it's important for the designer to maintain weekly meetings and communication with the production manager to ensure everything is runs smoothly. The designer should require a production manager or account person to oversee production and the process. At times the designer may need to send a person to oversee production on-site at the factory.

3.7   Quality Control

In the past, quality control in clothing manufacturing was primarily focused on final inspection, with a little 'in-process' inspection sometimes added. Increasingly, the focus has now shifted to the entire process to ensure quality at each of the various steps.

Quality control is the attention to issues that derive from the original design or the design of the production process itself. Responsibility for quality rests with inspectors rather than with the designers or production staff. Quality control is employed in the clothing industry where frequent design changes occur. This often causes a lot of rejects and requires an extensive repair system. It's useful to consider quality control as a cycle, in following areas.

1.   Study of customer requirements and definition of garment properties that define 'quality level'.

2. Satisfactory design, the degree of fit and range of sizes, seam strength, assembly, and wear ability.

3. Fabric, garment, and manufacturing specifications and requirements.

4. Ensure that manufacturing processes will meet the design requirements and that the machines used in production match the quality of the workmanship in the samples and that the designer has not created a feature so difficult to sew that maintaining consistency will be difficult.

5. Garment inspection and checks prior to shipping to ensure the execution of garments leaves no tears, stubs, hanging strings, or stains and has correct sizing.

6. Washing instructions ensuring proper care labels are available and that the care instructions are correct.

Production Planning Starts with Design

Too often, early-stage businesses don't create a production plan until it's too late and they find themselves with orders to fulfill and no one to produce them. It's important to identify production resources as soon as the samples production phase is complete, during your product development process. Your production and wholesale costs will then be based on real numbers even if your wholesale costs remain within a price bracket dictated by the market. With much competition for production vendors, it's essential to ensure you can secure production before investing time and money in the design process, sales process and on marketing.

3.8   **Steps to a Successful Production**

Regardless if you're producing overseas or domestically, production is essentially the same. Production is a process, with steps that must be followed. In order to ensure that production is successful, it's crucial for designers to follow these steps.

It takes time and experience to learn all that you need to know to manage production. Many factory owners and industry experts advise designers who want to have their own line to spend a few months in an internship or job at a factory. You need to know how to manage people, pinpoint problems, and identify mistakes. This is critical to learn how to manage a successful production. It's important for an organization to have someone who thinks like a manufacturer and for designers to know how clothes are produced.

When a designer has experience with the engineering and production process it is evident in the construction and quality of their garments.

Step 1: Define Your Product (pre-production)

Before starting to identify production resources, first decide what you are going to produce. Have your first samples, target costs (based on target wholesale costs), and spec sheets. You can contact production factories and manufacturers to get general ideas of their capacity, strengths, minimum quantities, and type of services offered but will not be able to get production quotes until you have a product to produce.

Step 2: Identify Production Resources and Develop a List

Given the competition between brands, production resources are often secret. It's important for a designer to develop their own contact list of resources and to keep adding to it. You never know when you may need an additional contractor.

There are many options for finding production resources. It's always a matter of leveraging relationships, being a good researcher, creative problem-solving, and keeping your eyes open. You may meet production people when you're not looking for them. Always get their contact info and check them out. Vendor and contact lists are considered confidential by many designers and wholesalers so you may not get a lot of information from industry people.

Step 3: Contact Manufacturers for Preliminary Production Quotes

Once you have product specs and a product, get production quotes and develop a short list of manufacturers you would like to pursue for production. This should be done in the sampling phase while creating a new collection. It's good to identify your production partner early in the process because their execution capabilities and associated costs need to be figured into your early design decisions and ultimately into the pricing.

Not all factories will have all the raw materials, fabrics and trims required to construct your product. If procurement falls on your company, you will need to source these yourself and incur costs that will likely need to be paid on an accelerated timeline.

Questions to ask potential factories:

- What services do you offer?

- What are your production minimums?

- Do you source fabrics and trim?

- What are your lead times for production? The lead time should include fabric and trim sourcing (if they're doing it) and the product assembly and finishing.

- What are your lead times for sourcing fabric? Manufacturers have different lead times for fabric sourcing that depend on their capacity. Depending on the fabrics used by other clients they service, they may be able to negotiate differently with fabric companies.

- What are your payment terms?

Step 4: Develop a Short List of Factories and a Timeline

As you're getting orders, develop a short list of factories that could work. You should have an idea about the fabric sourcing and if they will be able to do that for you or you will need to do it yourself. If you need to do the fabric sourcing, know when you need to start production and work backwards in the schedule so you know when fabric must be in production so the factory can get deliver on time.

Pre-Production Sample

You may want to have the factories sew a sample for you to demonstrate the quality of their work. Many overseas factories will do this. To get started with production, create or designate an approved sample as a template. This sew by sample or design prototype, is the model by which the factory will use to create bulk production. If an apparel company, use these samples to define construction guidelines, fit specifications and the grading of sizes up and down.

At this time, have a timeline with deadlines for ordering fabric (or approving fabric), ordering trim, and starting production.

Tech Packs

You should also start putting together the tech packs for production. Tech packs are the documents that contain all the relevant technical drawings and specifications such as, design style sheet, artwork, labelling, stitching details, and the colorways required for production and manufacturing of the garments. These documents need to show every detail and leave nothing to interpretation, as production may be made offshore where English is not the first language or spoken at all. Tech packs contain measurements, size specifications and garment measurements.

Step 5: Project Production Quantities Based on Orders

Project production quantities based on orders received. Do this early to determine how much fabric you need if you're ordering it. If the factory is sourcing the fabric and trim for you, you will need to request and approve swatches early enough for them to get it produced. This is also the time when you should get your finances in order to ensure you have the costs to pay for production deposits and the production completion.

Step 6: Order Fabric and Trim

If you must supply the fabric and trim, order it in time. If you are printing your own design on fabric or using a secondary fabric treatment like coating, you will need to order the fabric in time for it to be produced and the secondary treatment and printing to be completed before production begins. If you are producing yourself, you will likely have to pay some of the fabric cost upfront or give a deposit.

Sep 7: Start Production

Most suppliers will require some sort of deposit or prepayment to cover raw materials and the labor needed for production. The remaining balance will usually be required before the goods are ready to ship. Some suppliers will be flexible on terms, allowing you to delay these payments for weeks to months to support your cash flow as you will likely not be paid by your accounts or customers for some time. Always ask for terms so you can give yourself some cushion on payments and remember that whatever arrangements you agree on with your suppliers should always be captured in an official purchase order that details all the transaction and delivery terms. If the factory is sourcing all the materials, it's important to define the lead time from beginning to end and to give yourself a little room for delays to ensure you will make your ship date.

Step 8: Monitor Quality and Manage Communication

Once production is in process, monitor quality by comparing to the samples that buyers used to write their orders. The best way to do this is to visit the facility regularly. This is easier for domestic production but even for overseas production you'll want to see the products before they are shipped. Investing in this travel is critical. Depending on the situation, you may be able to conduct fittings on test or bulk units to make sure that they are executing correctly. If possible, this is highly advisable. If you are unable to visit your facilities, there are third party auditors that can oversee quality control for a fee.

Determine that the right amount of colors and quantity is produced per the retailer orders. Department stores and large retailers (including online retailers) will give you charge-backs for short-shipping or not shipping enough pieces, color substitutions, or shipping too many pieces.
If you have a problem with one style because something is not correct, notify the retailer as soon as possible and have the PO amended to ensure there is no charge-back.

Step 9: Retailer Packaging and Labelling Requirements

Ensure the retailer packaging and labelling requirements are met per their guidelines. This is a CRITICAL step that must be completed either at the factory, before the goods are shipped, or at your warehouse. You may want to communicate these requirements to your factory as part of the PO specifications. Department stores and larger retailers are very strict on the guidelines and failure to meet them will result in chargebacks and a lower profit margin.

Step 10: Shipping and Delivery

When goods are ready and approved for release you will likely have them shipped or delivered. Some companies will drop ship directly to their own retail stores or accounts and some will ship to a distribution warehouse or their offices. Once you take possession of the final products, you should pull some or all the units to check for quality on execution. This extra time and money is well spent when you consider the price of a customer or account returning any faulty or ill-fitting product. Have a clear understanding of any packing parameters required by specific accounts. Failure to adhere to these parameters can result in charge backs and even order cancellations.

3.9   Expertise and Specialty

Each factory has areas of expertise with the corresponding equipment and knowledgeable workers. Factories that excel at knits may not be able to produce outerwear or leather goods. Factories that are used to working with cotton or wool may not be competent with delicate silks. If a collection includes leather jackets, knit dresses, and woven pants, the designer may need to work with three different contractors.
Know what types of garments factories specialize in and their price levels. If they're doing mostly low-cost mass-merchandise garments and your garments are higher-costing contemporary garments, they may have the machines but not the experience to deliver what you want.

3.10   Types of Machinery Available and Production Services

Find out which production services the factory provides and whether they subcontract work out to others or do it all in-house. Many factories offer multiple services to attract more business, but subcontracted work is difficult to oversee. If you don't think the subcontractors can handle a process effectively don't give them the job.
Do they have all the grading technology and machinery? Do they have various sewing machines and needles needed for different fabrics?

3.11   Delivery

Ask if the factory regularly meets deadlines and establish the lead time for each job. Show your contact a sample or ask them to have one made one to help estimate timing as accurately as possible.
Inquire about the turnaround time for reorders. Reorders should be finished faster than the initial run.

Confirm what the factory means by delivery. To some, it may mean the product is just leaving the plant or is on a boat when what you need to know is when it will be in your possession. Determine what recourse you will have if the factory is late in delivering the goods.

3.12   Customer Service

Find out who you will deal with every day. How does the factory ensure quality at each stage of production? Ask the factory owner how to lower your costs and improve the production process.

3.13   Quality of Work

See some of the factory's finished work to analyze its quality. You might ask them to sample a garment if it makes sense. Ask the factory to make a finished production sample after you receive the cost estimate but before you give that factory the job. This will help you judge the quality of the work and help the factory owner provide you with an accurate price. Making a sample helps the workers understand the piece and it will give you a sense of what it is like to work with them. At this point they want your business and will be as responsive as they can be. Some factories, mostly overseas, will create the sample for free to try and secure your business, others will charge you three times the production price out of fear that you are using them just to get a sample.

3.14   Credibility

How long has the factory been in business? Who are some of its clients, and how long have they been clients? Call these clients for a recommendation.

Visit the factory and ask for a tour. Nancy Caton of Nancy Whiskey and the Sewing Factory advises, "Look for signs of good working conditions. Is the factory clean? Can you walk through it, or is the fabric stacked up to the people's shoulders? Do the people look happy?" If you doubt that the factory is legal, ask to see its business license and watch for signs of labor abuse.

How many employees are at the factory? Find out the factory's history of employee strikes and its policy if a strike causes production to stop.

What happens if your goods are damaged at the factory or during transport? What kind of insurance does the factory have?

3.15   Copyright Protection

Get a sense of how trustworthy the factory is regarding copyrights and private information. Probe the factory owner about other clients to see if the owner tells you things that he shouldn't. If proprietary details about another customer are shared, the owner will likely share the same information about you. Although there are steps to avoid some of this, it's hard to prevent a factory from taking a product and copying it. Only major brands can afford to do this and even they have a hard time preventing counterfeits.

3.16   Price and Payment Terms

Unfortunately, the cost of production often ends up being the last concern for a young designer. In the panic of finding the right materials, contracting quality production, and trying to get product delivered on time, a designer will pay almost anything.

Before you contract with a factory, it should give you an initial cost estimate made from the sample or spec sheet. The greater the quantity of items produced, the less each item will cost. Remember that everything is negotiable. If the price seems too good to be true, revisit any concerns about quality and delivery.

Generally, you will pay the factory COD, but often with a deposit of at least one-third of the price up front. Some factories require progress payments as the job passes through different stages of production. If a factory has had bad experiences with small designers, it's not unusual for them to demand full payment in advance.

If you pay fabric and production people on time, they will help you with discounts, better terms, flexibility on minimums, and other issues. The more work you give them, the happier and more supportive they will be in terms of price and service.

Pricing terms specify which party covers which parts of shipping. FOB includes the transportation to the shipping port but not the shipping, duty, or other costs from that point on. CIF includes shipping but not duty. When shipping fabric, ask for an LDP in which the shipping and duty is included in the quoted price.

3.17   The Production Agreement

The written agreement should include:

- The number and description of articles covered by the contract.
- Delivery date.
- Repercussions if delivery is late.

- Detailed finishing, packing, and labeling instructions according to the store requirements.
- The shipping method (local messenger, trucking, sea, or air).
- The payment due date and the method of payment.

Before you begin, confirm the number of units to be produced and which stages of production are being handled by which contractors. Also confirm that all samples, materials, and patterns will be returned to you. Be very clear about the delivery date. Larger jobs take priority at factories and despite the agreement, it's smart to give early deadlines to be safe.

Regardless of all this contract advice, not everything is written down. As one designer said, "Italian factories won't work with contracts unless your name is Prada, Gucci, or Ferragamo. You have to rely on the word of many people and be prepared for things to change without a moment's notice."

3.18   Funding and Partnership Potential

Increasingly, factories are looking to partner with smaller labels and even invest in their businesses. Many Chinese companies are seeking opportunities to continue their growth and increase their market shares and seek to partner, produce, and help fund new labels.

As larger manufacturers move production to Asia, Italian and other European factories are becoming more flexible, not just working with small labels but seeking to invest in them for increased efficiency, profit, and future loyalty. Manufacturers in places such as India often seek designers to create their own lower-priced lines and will partner to do your production in exchange for your design skills.

3.19   Full Package Production vs. Multiple Contractors

Production of garments can either be carried out in one place or between different places, each one specialized in a particular task. The choice between a full-package production and multiple-contractors production depends on the number of garments being produced and the size of the factory.

3.20   Advantages and Disadvantages of Full Package Production

Production can be simplified by choosing a vertical factory that offers multiple services such as fabric selection, patternmaking, production, and shipping in one place. Having fewer organizations involved means less opportunity for things to go wrong and processes to run late. The designer has more control when one factory handles many steps of the process and is more likely to provide accurate cost and timing estimates up front.

Consolidation results in efficiencies and savings. Factories that order fabric and trim place orders for multiple brands, resulting in bulk discounts, particularly with standard fabrics, such as denim, and performance fabrics for swimwear or active wear. Designers don't have to run to the factory every time it is short a button when the factory sourced the button and can order more.

Many overseas factories offer packages that include the entire process from sourcing and sampling to producing, finishing, and shipping the goods. Increasingly, in New York if you ask for a full package, the factory will comply. However, while packages make the production management job easier, some designers feel that packages limit the choice of materials and process too much and leave less room for maintaining quality standards and process control.

Advantages of Full Package Production:

- A designer can get everything done in the same place.

- Less resources to manage. Instead of managing a cutter, sewer, patternmaker/grader, and the material resources, a designer has less people to manage.

- Cost and time savings as here are generally cost savings when a factory does all the work.

Disadvantages of Full-Package Production

- Less room for changes. Once the production process starts, you may have less time to make changes and delay production which will disrupt the entire schedule and timeline. Often, if you cause any delays you will be placed in the back of the production queue.

- Less control. Depending on the size of your order, you may get bumped by a larger, more important order. You can ensure this doesn't happen by having solid dates scheduled into your agreements. You may have less day-to-day visibility and more periodic updating.

Many full-package factories with offices in the US do the production overseas. It's important to know where the production takes place and what production management resources are in place for managing it. We'll cover international full-package production in the next section.

3.21   Production Alternatives

In addition to full-service contractors, here are some production alternatives to consider.

In-House Production

Several emerging designers produce all or part of their line in-house with a small team. The team generally includes a patternmaker and several sewers. Obviously, this method can be very expensive and requires a significant outlay of funds for cutting, sewing, and pressing equipment, as well as the permits, insurance, and licenses legally required to run a production facility.

A designer I know with a very small in-house sewing room spends $20,000 a month to keep it running. She believes it's worth the extra expense because of the control it gives her. With in-house production, the designer can oversee the entire process every day and manage the timing and quality of each garment as it's produced. There is no competition from other designers and it's easy to react quickly for reorders and work around missing materials.

Designer Gustavo Cadile couldn't meet the minimums at the beading factories for his intricate evening wear gowns, so he manages an in-house team of extremely talented and experienced couture sewers who handle all his beading, sample production, and special orders.

Producing in-house results in a tight team of people who learn to work together efficiently, and the designer can train and teach the team to become experts in signature fits and finishes. Some designers take sewers on field trips to high-end stores to study the technique and finishing of different garments and set expectations.

An in-house sewing room can help protect proprietary information about design and fit. A designer told me she sends out her jackets, blouses, and dresses to a factory but will never contract out her pants. She has worked tirelessly to develop a signature fit and with many other jobs moving through the factories, she doesn't want to risk someone stealing her pattern.

In recent years, many New York factories have shut their doors, leaving a number of highly skilled workers out of a job. These are ideal people to hire for in-house production. Keep in mind, however, that even with your own in-house team, you won't have all the special skills required for each collection and will still have to contract out specialty work, such as beading or knitwear.

In-house production requires you to be there every day with the sewers, directing them and reviewing their work. Some designers who have an intense focus on quality are happy to spend all day measuring seams and checking finishes to ensure that each item is consistent. But not every designer wants the time-consuming responsibility of managing manufacturing processes and people.

A full-time production staff brings additional pressure. The sewers are employees and bring a serious financial obligation in terms of their salaries and benefits. You need to have the work to keep them busy and understand that you won't be the only one without a job if the business fails.

Freelance Sewers

If your orders are small or require special skills, individual sewers (or craftspeople) can be hired on a freelance basis to handle the production. Freelance sewers are expensive and generally take longer to produce but can be the best option when filling a one-time order for a store or creating specialty items that require detail or handwork. However, if you anticipate a large reorder or increased business with the store, you should get a factory involved to keep the production quality consistent on all runs and to provide quantity discounts and cost-effective measures.

Patch NYC started its business with a collection of crochet hats made completely by the mother of one of the designers and then embellished by designers John Ross and Don Carney. John says, "after one especially crazy crochet season, we realized Mom just couldn't keep up. We brought in two of Don's aunts and one of Mom's friends to help that season. Suddenly, there were all these variations in the hats since each person crochets slightly differently. We stopped wholesaling the crochet hats and only added knits back into our collection seasons later when we found a factory that would produce quality hats and scarves.

Nathalie —Alabama Chanin, the designer of Project Alabama, returned to her hometown of Florence, Alabama, to find quilting circles that could supply the handwork needed to produce her T-shirts. She supports the hometown economy by subcontracting to more than 100 women to do the stitching.

3.22   Producing Domestically vs. Off-Shore

One of the main production considerations is whether to produce domestically or overseas.

3.23   Domestic Production Advantages & Disadvantages

It's highly advisable to produce domestically or even locally if possible. The ability to oversee each process and communicate directly with people at the factory will make it easier to keep production on schedule and meet quality standards. You will also benefit from quicker deliveries to market and less danger of piracy that is often a problem with overseas factories. It may also be easier to negotiate terms when you are sitting in front of someone as opposed to on the phone or through email.

The downside of domestic or local production is that domestic labor costs are high, and you may not find a factory with the expertise you need.

While most small designers in the United States produce in New York, there are production opportunities everywhere. California is the largest producer of apparel in the United States. Driving your production around Los Angeles is easier than carrying it from block to block in New York.

There are designers in San Francisco, Dallas, Chicago, and Portland who produce in those cities and cite the advantages of working locally to produce specialized pieces and process quick reorders and small runs. Many smaller cities are working to support the local fashion industry by launching fashion weeks or creating programs that support designers.

Advantages of Domestic Production

- No customs duties, customs brokers, and associated costs. In some situations, this may mean saving as much as 28%-30% on the value of garment for some textiles. For example, if you're producing something overseas at $28, you must add a customs duty of 28% for jerseys and knits. This will cost you $35 plus overseas shipping cost of around $37. If you're produce this same item within the US, even with $35 in shipping, you will still save the international shipping cost. Of course, you must compare the units you would need to produce overseas to meet minimum with the minimum from the domestic factory.

- You save time as it takes about 2-4 weeks to ship goods by sea. It's a bit quicker through the air but is more expensive.

- Easier to do smaller quantities.

Disadvantages of Overseas Production

- Domestic labor costs are higher than foreign labor costs.

- There are not as many domestic factories and will have to compete with lots of other designers for the same resources.

- Domestic factories may not have the same machinery or resources as large foreign factories.

- No vertical integration and less access to sourcing partners that the factories have available.

3.24   International Foreign Production Advantages and Disadvantages

International, offshore production is often seen as a cheaper alternative. Most of the clothing sold in the US is made overseas which is largely due to labor costs.

Designers generally choose to produce overseas either for cost or quality reasons. Italian factories are credited with producing the highest quality of designer goods. They understand designer clothes and have highly trained craftspeople and artisans who have learned from generations of experts that take pride in their work. As a result, buyers are often more interested in items made in Italy.

Other countries have specialties as well. India is known for beading, Peru for knits, sweats in Canada and embroidery in Mexico, Turkey, Africa and the Caribbean. China has recently taken a large share of the market from these countries. Asia is known to have the cheapest production because of low labor costs.

In the last few years, China and Hong Kong have responded remarkably well to small companies. The myths that the factories in Asia are not interested in small designers and that their quality isn't as good is no longer true. There is a wide selection of factories in terms of size, quality, and expertise. There are factory owners who care about the quality and the vision for the product. Most emerging designers produce their knits in China because Chinese factories offer convenient packages and there are no longer as many knit producers in New York.

Recently, there has been some consumer backlash against goods produced in China which have impacted sales with certain groups of customers. Reports of high levels of toxins such as formaldehyde, in clothing and fabric, have created some apprehension about products made in China, especially in the children swear market.

There are challenges with communication, cost, timing, and quality when producing anywhere abroad.

There is a wide variety of fabric to choose from overseas. European mills are known for high-end quality fabrics, such as Italian cashmeres, as well as innovative and luxurious fabrics and prints. Japan has high-tech fabric, Korea has outerwear and synthetics, India has beading and silk, and China offers a large variety of inexpensive goods.

Most designers work with at least some imported goods. However, the extra shipping and duty costs, shipping delays, customs, and vacation times are issues to consider when working with overseas sources. Italian mills are closed for the entire month of August and Asia has several holidays which result in mills being closed for more than a week at a time. Long lead times can jeopardize delivery and the ability to fill reorders from the stores. For your first few seasons, buying overseas might not be worth the additional stress.

Advantages

Cheaper labor and materials costs.

- More resources available and better fabrics.

- More experience and/or higher degree of specialization in some techniques.

Disadvantages

- Harder to manage overseas production.

- Additional costs that need to be factored in that do not make it as cheap as initially thought of.

- Higher minimums required per order

- Language, cultural, communication issues.

- Overseas production requires tight management, great communication, and good time-management (allowing enough time).

3.25 Costs Associated with Offshore Production

When producing offshore, designers should remember the following production factors that add to production costs, labor, and materials.

Pricing terms specify which party covers the different costs of shipping. If the price is free on board (FOB), it includes only the transportation to the shipping port and not shipping, duty, or other costs after it leaves the port. Cost, insurance, freight (CIF) includes shipping but not duty. To avoid surprises, you should ask for landed duty paid (LDP) in which the shipping and all duty is included in the quoted price. However, many places won't ship fabric LDP and will leave the difficult task of calculating duty to you.

A customs broker or freight forwarder can help accurately estimate the shipping and duty. Brokers are paid a percentage of your total order. Although expensive, UPS or DHL can be used for shipping small quantities under tight time frames. These companies will handle customs and shouldn't take more than two to three days to receive fabric shipped from Europe by air.

Need to Check

1. How much of garment production is considered "made in x"? Some companies have tried going around various duties and quotas by having garments partially made elsewhere before shipping and finishing the last steps in the US in order to maintain the "Made in the US" label.

2. Countries specialize in particular manufacturing. For example, beading in India, sewing delicate fabrics and light-weight silks in China and Vietnam, cheap woven and leather manufacturing in Indonesia, etc.

3. Are there duties imposed on fabrics or materials imported into the country of manufacture if they're later exported to the US?

3.26 Warehousing Costs

Costs that affect the wholesale price of a garment are warehousing and storage costs. Clothing warehouses provide storage for garments, and oftentimes fulfillment of orders and shipping to retailers or consumers.

3.27 Customs and Duties Considerations

Customs duties can significantly affect the wholesale price of a garment and the resulting retail price. It's important to keep in mind the following to minimize duties.

3.28 Production Management and Quality Control when Producing Overseas

If you choose to produce overseas you need an agent or production manager whom you trust to oversee and manage production for you. Even if you have an agent or manager in that country you still may need to visit yourself. Without proper oversight, you can't ensure quality. In fact, you won't even know if the factory is outsourcing the production to another contractor. Have someone that speaks the language travel overseas to see production.

Designer Diego Binetti produces some of his womenswear line in China. His business partner, Ada Lee, is fluent in Chinese and travels to China for a month or more to oversee production each season. She goes to instruct the factory, explain the fit and stitching detail, and manage quality at every step in the process. If the factory in China makes mistakes that aren't caught before shipping, Diego uses a factory in New York for fixes. Being at the factory also led Ada to discover that the factory was using their pattern to make cheaper garments in different materials to sell as their own. This occasional shady practice can be stopped if someone is there to represent the designer.

Flying to the location for 24 hours to check on everything is not enough. Ideally, you need someone who is 100 percent on your side to be there all the time. Menswear designer Douglas Mandel of Kamkyl said the most frustrating thing for him about producing in Italy was being constantly pushed back by bigger manufacturers which resulted in his jobs being late.

Find a Production Agent You Can Trust

If being overseas for a long time to oversee production doesn't work, find a trustworthy production agent that is there all the time, to supervise production. They may need training but will be able to effectively represent you.

Check Quality Carefully and Frequently

When you inspect production, compare everything against the standard set by your production sample. Measure the seams, test that the buttons and labels are secure, and check that the stitching is straight. Look for color consistency and for stains from the machine oil or glue. Inspect the pressing and packaging. Inspect a number of items again before you pay at the end of production and refuse to pay if they're not up to standard. Change factories if the factory you are using can't get the quality right.

Fit Samples

If the factory is doing the grading, request to get fit samples for each style to make sure the grading has been well done and the sizes fit as required.

TOP's (Top of Production)

Before the production is completed, request the first pieces of production from each style to ensure that the production is of the required quality.

If you don't have someone to monitor production at the factory, have the factory send samples from multiple stages of the production run for your approval. Shipping will become a significant expense because of the constant back and forth but it's critical to guarantee good quality. Many Asian factories have very efficient and quick sample approval systems in place. Some visit New York each season to meet with their U.S. clients to review fabric and materials options and even test first samples.

3.29   Effective Communication is Crucial for Managing Production

Although communication may not directly affect profit margin it can indirectly have an effect. You may need to have a translator or local-language speaker, and communication limitations can cause delays or production problems.

3.30 Communication Considerations of Foreign Production

When you work with a factory, be specific and communicate clearly and often. Don't be afraid to ask questions but don't be difficult or annoying. You need the factory's partnership if materials are late or cutting tickets change during production because of new or revised orders. Know what you need before you call or show up and if you have a dispute or misunderstanding, sit down and work it out calmly.

Here are some common mistakes people make in communication, and how they could be avoided.

3.31 Avoid Common Communication Mistakes

Here are some common mistakes people make in communication and how they can be avoided. In many situations, communication issues are exacerbated by the language barrier and different styles of communication for specific countries and cultures.

Common Communication Mistakes

There are some specific communication principles to follow when you're communicating regarding production and finances. As a rule, it's always better to over-communicate than to under-communicate. Clear and effective communication will avoid time delays, mistakes, and unnecessary expenses.

Here are principles to use when communicating.

- **Be Specific:** Use order and product numbers even if you think it's obvious. What is obvious to you may not be as obvious to someone else who speaks a different language.

- **Use Clear Dates and Timelines**: Don't leave any information out.

- **Ask for Complete Information**:
  You get what you ask for and if you don't ask for what you really need, you will get an unclear and vague answer.

- **Specify the Action and Timeline Required:** If you need something done, specify what you would like done like fix something, send sample, or send info by a specific date.

- **Provide Quantifiable Information:** When dealing with specifications, provide specific measurements, color codes, etc. that the factory should base their action upon. Saying something is "too short" is not enough. You must tell them exactly what the expected and current length is and what they should do.

- **Take the Time to Communicate Well:** Many people think that saving time on typing is more advisable. In the day of mobile communication, many people tend to use abbreviations, cryptic sentences, and leave out information. You are communicating for money and anything that you leave out could cost you. Take the time to do it right.

- **Do Not Assume Anything:** Don't assume the reader of your communication knows what you mean. Even if you have had lengthy discussions with one person the message may be forwarded to someone else that doesn't know all of the particulars. Ensure everyone understands the same thing.

- **What is Your Objective?** Communicate your objective. If you want a specific outcome or action taken, ask for that action or outcome clearly and politely. Do not be ambiguous. If you need something to happen by a certain date say so and ask for a confirmation from them that they can do it. If you want a discount, ask for a specific figure. Ask if you can have a 20% discount rather than asking them to tell you the lowest amount they can give you.

- **Over-Communicate**: Even if it seems obvious and seems repetitive, it's better to over-communicate than to leave something out.

- **Use Clear Language as Opposed to Slang:** When communicating with factories overseas, you will be dealing with people who speak English as a second language and may not be familiar with the latest slang phrases. Production jargon is often difficult enough and different companies may refer to things by different names. If you are not sure about the terms they use, ask for clarification.

- **Request Confirmation and Send Confirmation**. When communicating on timely and important issues that have financial importance, confirm receipt of communication and ask for confirmation of receipt. This way people will know that you received their email. Likewise, by asking them to confirm receipt of communication, you will know that the email didn't go into their spam folder and was received by them.

3.32   Steps to Effective Communication with Your Factor and Team

Here are some steps to keep in mind when communicating with your production team and staff to effectively produce the results you are committed to producing.

1. Gather All of the Information

Know everything related to an issue such as the order number, style number, and the specific problem. It's easy to skip some of the specifics which will invariably lead to misunderstandings.

2. Decide on Outcome and Objective

What do you want to happen as a result of your communication? Don't assume anything. Don't assume that if you say you don't like something, they will know what to do exactly. What needs to happen and what and how does it need to be fixed?

3. Structure Your Communication to Clearly Address Each Question

If you have 5 questions, don't put them into a single paragraph. Number them clearly so they can answer each item separately. If you have multiple issues or corrections, make them easily identifiable. Use bullet points and short sentences. Make sure it's easy to read your communication.

4. Establish a Timeline

If you need answers by a certain date, ask for that date. When you specify that you will deliver or send something, specify when you will deliver it and keep your promise. When a package is sent ask for the estimated arrival day and time. When a production date is delayed, ask for a new date estimate.

5. Communicate towards a Solution and Keep it Positive

Placing blame will not solve a problem. Suggest a solution that will work for you. Keep emotion out of the communication even if it's hard and stressful and you're justified for being unhappy. Focus on the solution and be reasonable.

3.33   Production Quantities: Minimums for Fabric and Production

When dealing with production, your costs will depend upon your fabric and production minimums.

3.34   Fabric and Trim Minimums

Most suppliers of fabric and trim have a minimum amount of yardage (or meters in Europe) that designers can order. The minimums exist because, for the supplier, servicing, shipping, and selling small quantities is less profitable.

Each supplier has a different threshold of quantities. Minimums can range from 15 to 5,000 yards. Generally, for the designer fabric market, the average is around 300 yards. Certain fabrics from the same mill have different minimums depending on the content of the fabric, the finishes, or the print.

When you are new to the market and your orders are small, meeting minimums can be difficult. New designers do not need, nor can they afford, to buy excess quantities of fabric. When approaching any source for fabric or trim, determine the minimums up front. The question itself may expose you as someone not worth the supplier's time but it is a waste of your time to discuss materials you can't have. You don't want to fall in love with a sample fabric that won't be available for your orders.

3.35   If You Don't Meet Fabric Minimums

The reality is that new designers frequently cannot meet the minimums required by fabric suppliers. Don't despair, there are a few things you can do.

Buy Sample Yardage.

A supplier generally has two prices for fabric. One price is for sample yardage and is a higher price for a small amount of fabric. Sample yardage is used by designers to create a test sample for the design. Sample yardage can be 20% to 50% more than production yardage because the quantities are small.

The second price for production yardage is a lower price for larger quantities used to produce store orders. If you can't meet the required quantity for the production price, you can purchase the entire amount needed at the sample price. However, the cost will be high, and you risk the mill not working with you next season if don't return for a larger production quantity.

Pay More

Sometimes a source will make a minimum exception if you pay more per yard or pay a fee. This is generally a much better deal than paying the full sample yardage price. Many European mills have expensive couture lines of fabric and because the profit margin is higher for the mill, they sell that fabric in smaller quantities.

You can also negotiate with the supplier to find other ways to get past minimums or keep your price down. Ask them if a major manufacturer is buying the same fabric. If they are, you may be able to attach your order onto theirs.

Replace the Fabric with Something Similar

If you cannot find a company that makes the same fabric with a lower minimum, consider using a different fabric that has smaller minimums or offers in-stock fabric. You may keep the first sample with the high minimums in the line but require higher order quantities to meet minimums, with stipulations that it may get cancelled. Alternatively, if you absolutely must have that fabric, see where in the line you can use this fabric again for a sellable style in order to make the minimum order.

Buy Stocked Fabric

Ask the mill or supplier what fabric it has in stock. Most places house a selection of fabrics that require smaller minimums. If they don't stock exactly what you want, like black lace for example, they may have white lace you can dye. They also may have stock greige goods, which are unfinished goods that can be quickly dyed or treated. Ask whether they sell off leftover fabric at the end of the season. If you do buy stocked fabric, find out how much they have in total. If they run out, you may again face a 300-yard minimum to fill orders.

Be Creative

Designers find other clever ways to deal with minimums. For example, if you offer a shirt in four colors and the orders don't meet the minimums to buy the fabric in each color, you could buy the fabric for all of the shirts in white and dye it yourself, just make sure the fabric can be dyed.

3.36   Factory Production Minimums

Factories also require minimums because small production runs are time consuming and less profitable. When reviewing a factory, find out its production minimum and try not to waste time with factories that are not an option for you.

Find Production Minimums First

Many factories that specialize in small lots are at least open to negotiation, especially in New York and increasingly in Italy. More manufacturers are taking their production to Asia, forcing local factories to be more flexible and open to small companies. There are also companies in China that offer minimum quantities of 50.

Designers utilize several tricks to try to get around minimums but in a small industry, it's better to be straightforward and try to negotiate. If you don't meet the minimum, offer to pay more. For example, if the factory requires a 500-piece minimum at a price of $20 each, offer to pay $22 each for 250 pieces. If you negotiate this minimum up front and end up after market with orders for only 200 pieces, you will need to decide if you can take the loss on the extra 50 items or try to sell them elsewhere.

In general, extra stock simply ties up your money and you will likely have some returns and end up with extra inventory. Depending on the style, if that style was your best seller, having some pieces on hand for reorders may also be good. Never cut more than a 10% overage on your orders. If you can't sell enough to meet the factory minimum, it's best not to produce the piece at all.

There are options out there for selling off over-production and recouping your costs, these include in-season sales for immediate, online sales, flash sale sites, and off-price retailers.

Understand Definition of Minimum

Make sure you understand the definition of minimum. Some factories may have a minimum order of 200 per style but that may include all sizes and several color options.

Negotiate Minimums

When negotiating, try to convince the factory owner that working with you now will lead to a large production run in the future. Ask about the production capacity of the factory to imply that you are planning to have big volume soon.

It's important to pick your battles. If you negotiate minimums on all styles it may be difficult. If you have a few styles that are below minimum it may be easier. Remember, factories may negotiate minimums for a few styles, but will not do it for each style in the collection.

3.37   Minimum Production Quantities Affect Minimum Ordering Quantity

When looking at production order quantities, there are various minimums that depend on the manufacturer and type of production. The minimum quantities for production will determine your minimum order quantities that you will require from a buyer.

Minimum Order Quantities per Style and Color

The standard minimum order quantity per style and color is between 4 and 6 units for clothing in the contemporary market. If a brand is unknown and at a higher price-point, the minimum order quantity is closer to 4 units. If the wholesale price is lower, and the brand can be classified as a fast-fashion brand with a cash and carry business model, then the minimum will be 6 or 8 units pre-packed.

For example, a minimum quantity production of 200 pieces per style, will roughly mean 50 size runs (assuming 4 pcs in a size run, XS – L).

The production breakdown of quantities and sizes is set by specific ratios. For contemporary lines, a standard ratio for size breakdowns is 1-2-2-1, which translates to 1 XS, 2 S, 2M, 1L.

This would give you a production size breakdown as follows: 33 XS 66 S 67 M 34 L

The size breakdowns will ultimately be determined by the orders you receive. Retailers have a size breakdown based on consumer data which vary regionally and by clothing type. It's important to forecast your production and minimum quantities accurately. Then if you have additional product to sell beyond what you've ordered; you can take orders for immediate knowing what you will have available to sell.

Consider PFD Fabric and Small Dye lots for Basics

If you are producing basic styles that cross seasons and have a hard time meeting production minimum, consider using a fabric that's prepared for dyeing and dyeing the goods in small lots as needed. This works with cotton goods, t-shirts, and other goods where the style may not change as much from one season to another.

Over Production

It's not wise to plan to over-produce more than 10 percent on your orders. For example, if you have a minimum production quantity of 200, you should have orders for at least 180 pieces. You can then over-produce 20 more pieces and meet the minimum. In order to figure out what makes the most sense consider the cost of goods and the over-production needed.

The decision to over-produce is a function of the cost of production, wholesale profit margin, existing orders, and the type of clothing. If the clothing is basic, then over-producing some pieces may still allow the clothing to be sold through the next season, perhaps at a discount. If the pieces are very trendy, then over-producing could be risky and require a plan for selling overstock to off-price retailers or flash sales at a discount of 20% to 60%.

When to Over-Produce

You should only over-produce on top-selling titles with orders that can meet at least 75% of the production minimum. Here are some situations where it might be worth considering to over-produce.

- If you have orders for 80% of the minimum quantity and need to produce 20% to meet minimums.

- If your production costs are less than $20 per unit and you're making at least 50% profit (your wholesale is cost times two), and you are only over-producing 20-25% above the quantity ordered. This is worth considering if you can still make a marginal profit on pieces.

- You should not produce any styles in your collection that you didn't get orders for unless you can produce a small size run for your website. If you must order them, order as much as you think you can sell. You will be selling them at retail prices which will be more profitable.

- You should not, under any circumstance, produce the minimum quantity if you don't have at least 60% of the minimum order quantity on order.

How Much to Over-Produce

If you are planning on selling online through your website, depending on price-points, you should have 1 or 2 size runs available for your website. You should also budget 5 to 10 pieces as press giveaways to certain high-following bloggers in exchange for promoting your brand to their followers. Depending on your cost of production, the PR return on these giveaways may be significantly higher than spending thousands of dollars on a fashion show or spending $2,000 a month for PR services for 6 months.

You should never over-produce more than 25% of your orders and only for certain styles that will be easy to sell. Over-producing all styles across the line is too much of a risk.

When you sell over-production to an off-price retailer, you will likely need to sell it at a discount. This means that you will make a lower profit margin on those marginal goods. Off-price retailers are dealing with a conservative mass consumer and the pieces you over-produce must fit that clientele.

Ensure You Are Not Left with Stock

It's common for new designers to be over-optimistic about their sales and produce more than they can sell. Its best that a brand is not left with any stock and can sell everything they produce. There are several ways to make sure you're not left with stock.

Cut to order only. If you only cut to order you will not be left with any additional stock.

Pre-sell styles to off-price retailers to get an idea of what they would be able to take and at what prices. If you end up needing to over-produce on some styles, you'll know that you can sell those styles to them at the end of the season after you've shipped all of the other orders.

Continue to sell a style based on production units even after it has begun production. Communicate with your salespeople on a regular basis and send them reports of existing stock.

Adjusting the Initial Buy

You can use these options, if available, to adjust the initial buy. You may want to include some of these in your production agreements and pre-negotiate these with your manufacturer and fabric supplier.

Swing Quantity Option

You can make an advance commitment for fabric and garment production capacity with a clause that at a specified future date the quantity can be ordered up or down by 10% to 25%.

Switch Option

If a yard commitment is locked and cannot be changed, you may be able to switch the yarn from one knitting technique to another. For production, if you're using the same fabric for two styles and one of the styles is selling more than the other, switch the fabric to the better-selling one.

Sticking to Mill Goods

These are basic fabrics that are readily available that the mill can easily sell to others if you need to cancel an order. You should not stick to mill goods for everything as your line may not generate enough interest.

Sharing a Fabric

Using the same fabric for many styles allows you to switch it across to styles that sell better.

Sample Looms

If the woven mill allows smaller quantities for a fabric and you have to eliminate some patterns but keep the committed quantity, it may be faster to produce on smaller looms and get the fabric into production faster.

Staggered Trigger Dates

These are the final drop-dead dates by which production decisions must be made in order to meet production deadlines. Each individual decision is made as late as possible in the process to allow for the latest input and sales information.

Cancelling Styles

If the units ordered on a style are not enough, cancelling a style and offering the retailer something else as a substitute is a better option.

3.38   Shipping Product

Once goods are produced, shipping is the next important step in delivering the goods to the buyer. Since shipping happens at the end of the process, if there are delays pressure increases to ensure goods are not late. The shipping process starts after the final quality check is done and the goods are packed.

3.39   Order Shipping Process

Once goods are folded and packaged, the goods are packed according to retailer specifications.

Packing

Online retailers, department stores, and large retail chains will have their own specifications for packing goods. The specifications must be followed exactly to ensure the goods are shipped to the right distribution center and shipping mistakes do not incur chargebacks.

Retailers, especially department stores, have specific packing and shipping instructions that must be followed, or they will refuse the goods or issue chargeback fees.

Read the routing guide from the store thoroughly and follow the directions. Packing details will tell you if the garments should be on hangers or packed flat in bags, wrapped in plastic, or tagged in a specific place with specific information.

Shipping instructions indicate the shipping method that should be used, the documentation and packing slips required, and the format for labeling the boxes. Don't forget to order packing materials in advance. While some of these requirements seem overly demanding, the stores receive thousands of items each day. To get your goods onto the selling floor quickly, the box labels, packing slips, packing bags, and hangtags must provide all the information to help the stores quickly process the boxes and items. They should be able to tell the style name and number, size, color, and even the neckline style or sleeve-length without unpacking or unfolding each item.

At most small companies the designers and their staff personally pack and ship the goods. It's an ideal time to connect with each product and verify quality standards have been met. The designer can control the packing process and make sure that directions from the stores are carefully followed.

Take your time and pull each order one at a time. Confirm whether the shipment is insured by the shipper or the retailer. Once shipped, track the deliveries. When shipping small amounts overseas, FedEx, DHL, or UPS can act as a customs broker. Once you start shipping in volume, it's preferable to use a freight forwarder or fulfillment service that can help with paperwork and international shipping regulations, book the shipping, arrange for insurance, and save money through consolidation.

Packing Slip

The packing slip must match the retailer's invoice. The retailer invoice must match the PO for the pieces ordered. If there's a discrepancy between the packing slip and invoice the invoice doesn't get paid by the retailer. The packing and shipping department from the factory's warehouse, or the designer's warehouse, arranges the transportation of the garments from the factory to the retailer's warehouse.

Cartons & Freight

Depending on retailer specifications, some garments may be shipped on hangers (GOH) or packed into cardboard cartons. If the garments are expensive, it may be advisable to ship these garments in a wardrobe box (hanging on a rod in a box). Most cartons shipped by sea get packed into containers that are 20 or 40 feet long and placed onto pallets that are consolidated into larger shipments. It takes up to 60 days for sea freight depending on the origin city and destination. If goods are shipped by plane, they are generally sent as air freight and consolidated into other larger shipments. Air freight may take less time but be more expensive.

Commercial Invoice and Shipping Documentation

The shipping documentation is prepared by the factory and includes a customs declaration, commercial invoice and other shipping documents. The commercial Invoice may list prices different than the actual prices depending on the declared values for customs. The customs declaration will include the following:

- Type of garment (men's, jacket, outerwear, etc.)
- Fabric content
- Number of pieces in each size
- Any additional materials (i.e. buttons, etc.) that may be important

It's important the customs declaration is well done, or the goods will be stuck in customs at arrival and cause delays. The designer should have a reputable customs clearing agent to ensure goods pass through customs quickly. Paperwork should be sent to the US Customs clearing agent as soon as it's prepared for review and to spot any potential problems.

Arrival and Customs Clearance

Upon arrival in the US, the goods are stored until they have cleared customs. Clearing customs includes payment of customs duties and applicable fees. Airlines and shipping companies only allow a short time for custom clearance before they start charging storage fees. It's important for designers to have the customs clearing agent ready to process as soon as the shipment arrives.

Delivery of Goods

Once goods have cleared customs they are taken from the airport or port location to the warehouse or fulfillment center. In some cases, the goods may be directly shipped to the retailer.

Fulfillment Centers

At some point, you will want to work with a fulfillment center rather than handle all of the tagging, shipping, and packaging of product in your own studio. As volume grows, shipping becomes too time consuming and complicated and takes up too much space. When selling to department stores it is critical to work with a fulfillment center to meet all the vendor compliance requirements correctly and avoid chargebacks and returns.

Fulfillment centers offer a range of services and capabilities and you can negotiate a package based on your business needs. They will charge you for storage, shipping and other services you have selected. A fulfillment center may offer warehousing and inventory management, garment on hanger (GOH) shipping, pick order or batch order processing (assembling mixed orders of items that arrive from different manufacturers for shipping to multiple customers), processing returns, customs clearance, hang tag and price ticket application, credit checks, invoicing, and a range of barcode and EDI-compliant services.

3.40   Shipping Window

In order to account for shipping delays, it's important to add additional time into the schedule prior to the retail cancellation date to ensure goods arrive on time.

30 Day Shipping Window

Knowing that almost anything can delay production or shipping, designers should have a 30-day cushion between the planned arrival to the warehouse and the start-ship date for the retailer. This window is extra important if you are using different contractors to make specific styles since you will need to ship all of the styles together to the retailer.

Retailer Shipping Window

Retailers also have a shipping window of 30 days. The shipping windows generally goes from the end of one month the end of the next month. This is the time the shipment must be complete or cancelled. Smaller specialty stores are more lenient with their cancel dates. Department stores will generally request an additional discount for shipments requesting a shipping extension date of over 3 days.

3.41   Partial Shipments, Back-Orders & Short-Shipment

Depending on the retailer, there may be different rules regarding orders that are not shipped complete. They may include partial shipments, back-orders, and short-shipments.

Partial Shipments

Partial shipments are shipments of styles done separately as they become ready rather than after everything is complete. In some situations, retailers prefer that the styles ship as they are ready and arrive in a staggered order rather than all at once. This depends on the styles ordered and merchandising of the styles ordered.

Back Orders

Back-orders may occur when ordered goods have sold out and are on order. Retailers may also do a back-up order for additional units they think they will need to re-order in advance. This ensures they receive the back-ordered goods before the projected time they expect to run out of the ordered product.

Short-Shipment

Short shipments occur when the shipped quantities of the goods are less than the original quantities ordered by the retailer. Some retailers may only allow for a certain amount of short-shipments or may institute chargebacks for short-shipments. It's important for designers to ensure they're not short-shipping or over-shipping goods.

3.42   Shipping on Time is Crucial

Shipping on time will ensure that orders are received, and designers are paid on time and stay in business. Shipping on time is mandatory with both large retailers and online retailers who are very strict with cancellation dates. The larger the order the more stringent the cancellation date.

Designers generally have a 30-day shipping window to start shipping and complete the shipment of their product. This means the shipment cannot leave their warehouse earlier than the start-ship date and must arrive before the cancellation date (also called the end-ship date). Production must be tightly managed at all stages to ensure timely shipment.

Count backwards from the end ship date to create the various deadlines by which certain steps of the production process need to be completed. If you count backwards between the end start ship date and completion of production, you will see 30 days. Production generally takes four weeks which adds an additional month as does fabric which additional four to six weeks. In other words, to meet deadlines, it order fabric two months from the end of production and three months prior to start ship date for a retailer.

Due to these production delays, designers need to be very focused on a strong sales effort as the selling window to get a maximum of orders is quite tight (about 2-3 months).

Fabric and Trim Shipping

Fabric must be shipped before garment production begins. It may take 30 to 60 days for fabric to be produced. This time must be accounted for in the schedule. Fabric shipping may also add additional time although most fabric is shipped by air.

Manufacturing: Allow Time for Sample Approvals

Another potential time delay can happen during the manufacturing process as samples are created and sent for approval. It's important to plan for these sample reviews and approvals. Without approvals it is difficult for an overseas designer to ensure that the goods produced match what the retailer ordered.

Shipping Timeline

If manufacturing overseas and shipping by sea a shipment will take four to six weeks. Air shipments may take only a week.

Customs Delays

Additional delays can be caused by customs clearance if the paperwork is not filled correctly or there are discrepancies. Sometimes designers declare the fabric very carefully but forget about the notions and trim. In some situations, specifying the materials or the fiber content of the notions and trim will ensure there are no customs delays.

3.43   How to Avoid Shipping Delays

The best ways to avoid shipping delays is through careful planning and detailed information.

Adjust Shipping Window

If the shipping date is too tight according to production timelines, avoid being late by negotiating a wider shipping window with the retailer. For example, negotiate 1.5 months instead of a 1 month start ship date. An additional 15 days will often be enough of a cushion.

Constant Communication with Factory

It's important to communicate with the factory constantly. If anything runs late, even a few days, it may be necessary to adjust the start ship date early in the process instead of hoping to make up time in the course of production, so the shipment is delivered when promised.

Getting Payment Information Confirmed Prior to Shipping

Another common shipping delay happens from not getting payment information confirmed for credit card orders and credit card orders being unable to be processed. It's important to get credit card information confirmed 1 month prior to start-ship date. In some situations, fraud controls will prevent the credit card transaction from being processed. Be sure to notify the buyer prior to shipping so they are aware of the credit card transaction and can notify their bank.

3.44   Private Label Production

For many designers, private label can be a profitable option. It's an indirect method of sales that is increasingly used by more retailers. Every retailer seems to have their own private label.

Private label programs essentially eliminate the role of the wholesaler. Someone still must decide about the styling of the merchandise and this decision is ultimately owned by the retailer rather than the designer. Private label lines are usually less daring than designers' lines.

Merchandise must still be produced but with a private label the production tasks are performed by individuals who work directly for the retail store. They don't need to promote their line to a buyer because they are the buyer.

3.45   How Private Label Works

The retailer commissions manufacturers to develop and produce special merchandise for their store. The merchandise has the store's own label sewn into the garment.

Private label is big business and continues to grow with retailers. It can be done by brick-and-mortar retailers, catalog retailers selling via catalogs (now online), or through other media like QVC.

Private Label - Two Types

There are normally two types of private label.

1. Developed to look like designer or branded clothes.

2. Developed to be constructed cheaper like a bargain brand.

Private Label as Incentives for Department Stores

Manufacturers are concerned by the private label trend because it excludes their own product. However, to keep contact with the department stores, manufacturers agree to include a certain percentage of their product as private label. In exchange, the retailer agrees to carry the manufacturer's own label. In effect, the manufacturer is forced to be the contractor for the retailer!

"Virtual Vertical Retailers" are successful retailers who have created their own design, product development, sourcing, and delivery organizations to implement their other traditional contacts with manufacturers. Target, Kmart, and Walmart all have their own private labels that play a significant role in their purchasing power.

Manufacturers throughout the world create product for Banana Republic, Ann Taylor, Martha Stewart, Urban Outfitters. Manufacturers offer packaged, private labels selling directly to the retailer or by selling through a brand names like Nike, Cherokee, Victoria Secrets, etc.

Becoming a successful private label manufacturer demands knowledge of the brand and the trends in the market, an understanding of the product development process, and an ability to deliver a product on time.

3.46 Private Label Production vs. Producing Your Own Brand

For private label, the number of steps required is fewer than in the traditional process. This results in a streamlined process and the retailer saves money. Private-label merchandise is more profitable for retailers.

The private-label item can be produced at a lower overall cost than a designer brand or national brand item of identical quality. The elimination of steps doesn't mean a lower product quality. Usually retailers who do private label will pass some of these savings to consumers and offer them greater value. Both the consumer and the retailer profit in this situation.

Private-label only stores exploded during the 1990's. Gap, Limited, Ann Taylor, J. Crew, Abercrombie & Fitch are some of the best examples. The unified vision and control of the product, the store environment, and advertising have allowed them to project strong brand images.

Private label programs are now huge. Between specialty chains and department stores, NPD Research group estimates that in 1998 private label accounted for 32% of total women's apparel sales in the US.

There are essentially two types of private labels. One for stores that carry only their private label merchandise, and another for stores that carry designer and national brands in addition to their private label.

The second type of private label, which carry designer and national brands, are exclusive to the store. Merchandise can only be bought in the store that owns the label while other brands can be bought elsewhere.

Most department stores also aggressively pursue private label to counter the dominance of the more powerful wholesalers' brands. Retailer private label brands don't have as much of a strong brand identity as the private-label-only brands. The common assumption in the industry is that department store assortments are approximately 15% to 20% private label. For discount stores, the percentage of private label is even larger.

3.47   What to Consider When Selling Private Label

Sometimes the promise of many units and increased profits is so attractive to a manufacturer that they don't consider the impact of private label on their own brand and business. If the retailers are buying your product private label and can get the same quality and styling for less, why should they buy your product at a higher price?

Interactive TV contracts may require a lot of units but don't have guarantees and may not pay in the end. It's important for the designer to make decisions that will not drive down their business.

A designer should do private label only if it makes sense for them strategically and production won't require a different direction that requires additional development.

Also, keep the private label goods sufficiently different from branded merchandise. This way, if the private-label goods are selling next to the branded goods it will not hurt the brand.

3.48   Advantages of Private Label

Exclusivity

This is probably one of the most important reasons. If no one else carries these items, you don't have to put yours on sale the minute your competitor does. As a designer, there may be little room for a higher profit margin.

More Units Sold

Private label, thought it may be cheaper, may allow the designer to sell more units and create greater revenue. Private label may also bring a lower profit margin and lower cost requirements. Designers need to assess if it really makes sense for them to do private label.

3.49   Disadvantages of Doing Private Label

There are some disadvantages for the designer to do private label for a retailer.

Less Original

Generally, private-label merchandise is usually less original and less daring. Customers trust private labels to give them the courage to try something new. Because of the cost-commitment involved, retailers only develop private-label items they know will be big sellers. Items in a private-label line are often close interpretations of those that have already sold well from higher-priced branded lines. For example, Macy's INC private label brand, positioned as better update, would take strong direction from the designer and bridge update vendors such as Prada, Gucci, DKNY, Calvin Klein. Private-label product development is more creative than simply copying someone else's style but less original than creating a new style from scratch.

Private-label brands can also be designed and merchandised with the help of a designer. The designer takes their collection and designs exclusive styles for the retailer, designs that are not sold anywhere else. The fabrics and styles are sometimes adjusted to fit the retailer's price-point. Depending on the situation, the designer may keep their name on the label or not.

Can Hurt the Brand Image

Depending on the required cost and quality, private label can negatively impact the brand image if there's too much of a difference in quality between your brand and the store's specific brand. If the difference in price and quality is too high, it may be better for the designer not to have their name on the product if their brand identify is not strong enough.

3.50   EDI

Electronic data interchange (EDI) is the electronic exchange of information between two computers. Most department stores require vendors to be EDI compliant and to use barcode technology on their shipments. Department stores receive thousands of items each week and must organize and process them quickly to get them onto the selling floor. It is generally too expensive for a newer designer to invest in this technology, so you should ask for an exemption from a department store for the first few seasons. However, if a fulfillment center has the EDI and barcode software, you will be able to comply earlier without making the investment yourself. As a result, the stores will get your goods onto the floor more quickly, allowing them more time to sell at full price and avoiding the expensive charge backs that result from packing and shipping errors.

Important Things to Consider with EDI

Make sure your fulfillment company has insurance and that it is EDI-compliant and can meet the requirements of your department store clients. Ask what discounts it has with the major shipping companies, such as UPS and FedEx and how fast it can turn around orders and shipments. Ask if it offers same day shipping.

Make sure you get training on EDI to understand the process and how to work with it. Having everything done correctly will ensure you don't get chargebacks.

3.51   Production Do's and Don'ts

Do's

- Review your production schedule monthly and adjust.
- Weigh the costs of producing overseas vs. domestic production, including fabric sourcing process, and the additional resources the factory has available, vs. the schedule and cost.
- Continue to add to your list of production resources.
- Produce only the styles you think you will be able to sell, through the various sales channels.

Don'ts and Common Mistakes

- Don't fully trust a factory even if they're completely trustworthy. Check up on them periodically and do your homework. They may be well-intentioned, but it only takes one mistake to ruin an entire batch. One bad employee can be the undoing of your production run.

- Don't assume anything. Communicate as if everyone needs the issues explained fully from the beginning. Don't assume that anything is ok until you've inspected it yourself.

About the Author - Lisa Elliot-Rosas

Lisa began her career working with brands in-house and a variety over 25 years ago. She has worked in product development, marketing, press, merchandising and sales.

In 2001 she began eM Productions in Los Angeles. A few years later she opened up a NY showroom.

The company began with press and producing shows. In 2005 began focusing strictly on sales and branding.

Over the years, eM Productions turned several unknown designers into known brands and with strategic sales, marketing and partnership was able to grow. Some key lines were Mara Hoffman, Ace and Jig, Veda, Iro, Zadig and Voltaire, amongst others.